Intangible Capital and Rates of Return

Effects of Research and Promotion on Profitability

Kenneth W. Clarkson
With a foreword by Yale Brozen

American Enterprise Institute for Public Policy Research
Washington, D.C.

Kenneth W. Clarkson is a professor of economics at the Law and Economics Center, University of Miami School of Law.

Library of Congress Cataloging in Publication Data

Clarkson, Kenneth W
    Intangible capital and rates of return.

    (AEI studies; 138)
    1. Profit—Accounting.   2. Monopolies.
3. Intangible property.   4. Drug trade—United States—
Finance. I. Title. II. Series: American Enterprise
Institute for Public Policy Research. AEI studies; 138.
HF5681.P8C6   658.1'554   77-948
ISBN 0-8447-3235-4

AEI Studies 138

Printed in the United States of America

Intangible Capital and Rates of Return

CONTENTS

Appendixes

Tables

FOREWORD

A multitude of studies, seeking to identify the consequences of industrial concentration, of advertising, of regulation, of collusion, and of the costs to society of monopoly effects on the allocation of resources, have relied on accounting rates of return as a measure of these consequences. The accounting rate of return suffers from a number of deficiencies, however, which make it an unreliable indicator. Kenneth W. Clarkson, in this study, presents corrected rates of return for eleven industries which, while not eliminating all sources of deficiency, take us part of the way down the road we should travel before doing monopoly studies.

The following excerpts from Fritz Machlup's 1952 treatise on the political economy of monopoly attest to the importance of Professor Clarkson's undertaking:

> Although many monopolistic firms may make profits, there are several fundamental pitfalls in the idea that the accounting rate of profit can show the degree to which monopoly power is exercised.
>
> That the accounting rates of profit, the only ones that may be available to the statistician, are such unreliable indices of economic excess profits and monopoly situations is unfortunate, since the relationship between supernormal profits and monopolistic barriers against potential entrants into the industry is highly significant. Firms sheltered against newcomers' competition are likely to earn higher returns on their investments than firms in industries wide open to anybody willing to start a new business.
>
> Before results of investigations of "adjusted profit rates" become available we cannot say whether and how it will be

1

possible to separate monopoly elements. But we know for certain that such a separation is not possible on the basis of the unadjusted accounting rates of profit and that these rates cannot be accepted as a measurement of the degree of monopoly.[1]

In his investigation, Professor Clarkson has paid special attention to the pharmaceutical industry because it appears to have been very profitable in comparison with other industries. Using accounting rates of return on net worth as a measure of profitability, the First National City Bank (FNCB) has, during the last twenty-five years, consistently ranked the drug industry in the upper fifth of the industries on its list.[2] The Federal Trade Commission (FTC), tracking a different set of industries, has consistently ranked pharmaceuticals in the upper fourth.[3] In more years than has been the case for any other single industry, this industry has ranked number one in both groups.

If high or low profitability for an industry is the result of competitive disequilibrium, we should expect those with a high rank in any year to descend and those with a low rank to ascend toward a middle rank in later years. Additional resources will be attracted to high-return industries, causing capacity and supply to rise and prices and profits to fall. Capital will be repelled by low returns, and prices and profits will tend to rise in low-return industries. Also, the resources required to maintain equilibrium will change randomly relative to the total resources put into the various industries, unless there is greater-than-average growth in the demand for an industry's product. If growth is consistently underanticipated, an industry may enjoy persistent above-average returns.[4]

History provides examples of the convergence phenomenon. Take two comparably prosperous years such as 1948 and 1956. In 1948, the twenty industries in the upper half of the forty shown in

---

[1] F. Machlup, *The Political Economy of Monopoly* (Baltimore: Johns Hopkins Press, 1952), pp. 493, 495, and 497.

[2] Annual reports on rates of return earned by leading manufacturing corporations aggregated by industry, published in April issues, 1951-1976, of the *First National City Bank Monthly Economic Letter.*

[3] *Report of the Federal Trade Commission on Rates of Return in Selected Manufacturing Industries* (Washington, D.C.: U.S. Government Printing Office, various years, 1954-1973).

[4] For an amplified discussion of these points, see George J. Stigler, *Capital and Rates of Return in Manufacturing Industries* (Princeton: Princeton University Press for the National Bureau of Economic Research, 1963), pp. 3-6.

Table 1 had an average rank of 10.5. These twenty industries fell in average rank in the next eight years, ending in 1956 with a random distribution among the forty ranks and an average rank of 19.6—just what we would expect if industries are indeed competitive.

If we rank industries by rate of return in 1956, as in Table 2, we find the 1948-1956 convergence of upper and lower rank industries repeated in 1956-1966. Both 1956 and 1966 were prosperous years, which means that it was not the differential cyclical sensitivity of profits in different industries which mixed ranks.[5] The average rank of the more profitable half of the industry list fell from 10.5 in 1956 to 17.4 in 1966. The average in the less profitable half of the list rose from 30.5 to 23.6. Again, we would expect this in a group of competitive industries.[6]

A few industries are notable for their persistence in the lower or upper quartiles of these lists of industries. Meat packing ranked thirty-ninth in 1948, next to the bottom of the list. It remained at approximately the same rank in 1956 (thirty-seventh) and in 1966 (fortieth). Sugar was in the bottom quintile in 1948 and remained there in 1956 and 1966. Drugs and medicines were in the number one position in 1956 and slipped only to third rank in 1966. Office equipment, soap and cosmetics, and instruments and photographic goods were in the upper quartile in 1956 and repeated that performance in 1966.

If the ranks of industries in one prosperous year are not correlated with their ranks in another prosperous year eight to ten years later, can chance alone account for the fact that a few industries persist in top or bottom groups? It has been suggested that the persistence of some industries in a top rank must be the consequence of monopoly in those industries.[7] Presumably, bottom-ranked industries persist in those ranks because they operate with very long-lived assets specialized to those industries and the demand facing them fails to grow with the growth in population and per capita income (or fails

---

[5] To the extent that an industry is cyclically sensitive, with high returns in prosperous years and low profits in depressed years, we should expect it to be in the high-ranking group in almost all prosperous years.

[6] See note 5, above, for a reason not to expect a completely random redistribution of the ranks of high-ranking industries when comparing one prosperous year with another.

[7] For example: "the persistence of high profits over extended time periods and over whole industries . . . suggest artificial restraints on output and the absence of fully effective competition." White House Task Force on Antitrust Policy, Report 1, *Trade Regulation Report*, supplement to no. 415 (May 26, 1969), p. I-9.

Table 1
RETURN ON NET WORTH IN LEADING MANUFACTURING CORPORATIONS AND RANK BY INDUSTRY GROUP, 1948 AND 1956

Number of Firms in 1948 by Industry	Return on Net Worth (in percentages)		Rank by Return	
	1948	1956	1948	1956
29 Lumber	29.3	12.6	1	20
45 House appliances	26.6	12.1	2	25
28 Automobiles and trucks	26.0	14.6	3	12.5
12 Distilling	24.8	6.8	4	38
27 Office equipment	24.3	17.5	5	7.5
68 Automotive parts	23.5	13.3	6	19
31 Brewing	22.8	8.1	7	35
44 Petroleum products	22.1	14.6	8	12.5
24 Baking	21.4	12.2	9	22.5
32 Drugs, soap, cosmetics	21.3	19.9	10	4
77 Building and plumbing equipment	21.0	11.2	11	30
7 Woolen goods	20.9	6.6	12	39.5
17 Soft drinks	20.4	14.3	13.5	14
85 Pulp and paper	20.4	13.8	13.5	16.5
80 Electronic equipment, radio, television	20.3	11.8	15	27.5
166 Machinery	18.6	14.9	16	11
18 Furniture	18.3	11.8	17	27.5
45 Other stone	18.2	15.8	18	9
65 Chemicals	17.7	15.5	19.5	10
94 Other metal products	17.7	12.1	19.5	25
31 Cement	17.0	20.6	21	2
82 Other food	16.9	11.7	22	29
47 Hardware and tools	16.3	12.2	23	22.5
13 Glass	15.5	17.7	24	6
34 Nonferrous metals	14.9	17.8	25	5
25 Shoes	14.7	10.3	26	32
34 Printing and publishing	14.3	13.8	27.5	16.5
23 Tobacco products	14.3	12.1	27.5	25
25 Tires, rubber products	14.0	13.6	29	18
54 Iron and steel	13.9	13.9	30	15
33 Apparel	13.8	7.8	31	36

Table 1 (continued)

Number of Firms in 1948 by Industry	Return on Net Worth (in percentages)		Rank by Return	
	1948	1956	1948	1956
12 Agricultural implements	13.6	8.3	32.5	34
9 Leather	13.6	10.8	32.5	31
19 Paint	13.1	17.5	34	7.5
18 Dairy products	13.0	12.4	35	21
23 Sugar	12.2	6.6	36	39.5
6 Shipbuilding	11.7	20.0	37	3
27 Railway equipment	9.2	9.9	38	33
21 Meat packing	7.2	7.7	39	37
27 Aircraft	2.9	21.4	40	1
TOTAL	18.2	13.9		

Note: The average rank of the industries may be summarized as follows:

	Average Rank	
	1948	1956
Industries 1–20 (1948)	10.5	19.6
Industries 21–40 (1948)	30.5	21.4
All industries	20.5	20.5

Source: *First National City Bank Monthly Economic Letter*, April 1949 and 1950 and April 1957 and 1958.

to grow rapidly enough to offset the rise in cost of variable inputs used with specialized durable assets).[8]

[8] There is evidence indicating that the apparent persistence of meat packing at a low rank must be the consequence of inadequate data used in the FNCB report. The fact that a large number of firms was attracted by this industry and entered it suggests that the rate of return was attractive and that the use of rates of return for only the leading firms (which is the case in the FNCB report) does not properly represent the average rate of return earned by the whole industry. The number of firms in meat packing increased from 1,999 in 1947 to 2,529 in 1967. U.S. Bureau of the Census, Census of Manufactures, 1967, Special Report Series: *Concentration Ratios in Manufacturing* (Washington: U.S. Government Printing Office, 1970), p. SR2-7. The FNCB reports used fifteen to twenty-one leading meat-packing corporations. Ralph C. Epstein, *Industrial Profits in the United States* (New York: National Bureau of Economic Research, 1934), pp. 248, 273, reports that while twenty-three leading meat-packing firms earned only 1.9 percent on equity in 1928, forty-six minor meat-packing firms earned 10.0 percent. Leo Troy, *Manual of Performance Ratios for Business Analysis and Profit Evaluation* (Englewood Cliffs, N. J.: Prentice-Hall, 1966), p. 293, reports that meat-product firms with assets under $500,000 earned 13.6 percent on net worth in 1964 while firms in this industry with assets of more than $50 million earned only 3.7 percent.

Table 2

RETURN ON NET WORTH IN LEADING MANUFACTURING CORPORATIONS AND RANK BY INDUSTRY GROUP, 1956 AND 1966

Number of Firms in 1956 by Industry	Return on Net Worth (in percentages)		Rank by Return	
	1956	1966	1956	1966
24 Drugs and medicines	21.9	21.0	1	3
41 Aircraft and parts	21.4	15.7	2	12.5
30 Cement	20.6	7.0	3	39
46 Nonferrous metal	17.8	15.7	4	12.5
18 Glass	17.7	12.7	5	28
22 Paint and varnish	17.5	13.9	6.5	21.5
27 Office equipment	17.5	18.1	6.5	5.5
77 Instruments, photo goods	16.3	21.2	8	2
22 Soap, cosmetics	16.2	17.9	9	7
55 Other stone	15.8	9.2	10	37
69 Chemical	15.5	15.1	11	14
168 Machinery	14.9	16.0	12	10
14 Automobiles and trucks	14.6	17.8	13.5	8
116 Petroleum products (and refining)	14.6	12.6	13.5	29
15 Soft drinks	14.3	22.0	15	1
56 Iron and steel	13.9	9.3	16	36
73 Paper	13.8	11.8	17.5	33
42 Printing and publishing	13.8	18.1	17.5	5.5
29 Tires, rubber products	13.6	13.0	19	26
57 Automotive parts	13.3	14.5	20	17
26 Lumber and wood products	12.6	11.0	21	34
12 Dairy products	12.4	12.4	22	30
18 Baking	12.2	13.9	23.5	21.5
51 Hardware and tools	12.2	19.2	23.5	4
36 Household appliances	12.1	15.0	26	15
112 Other metal products	12.1	14.0	26	20
20 Tobacco products	12.1	13.8	26	23
19 Furniture	11.8	14.2	28.5	18.5
97 Electronic equipment, radio and television	11.8	16.7	28.5	9
88 Other food	11.7	13.3	30	24
81 Building, heating and plumbing equipment	11.2	11.9	31	31.5

Table 2 (continued)

Number of Firms in 1956 by Industry	Return on Net Worth (in percentages)		Rank by Return	
	1956	1966	1956	1966
25 Shoes, leather	10.3	13.1	32	25
21 Railway equipment	9.9	14.2	33	18.5
10 Agricultural implements	8.3	14.7	34	16
24 Brewing	8.1	12.8	35	27
49 Clothing and apparel	7.8	15.9	36	11
15 Meat packing	7.7	5.5	37	40
12 Distilling	6.8	10.6	38	35
80 Textile products	6.6	11.9	39.5	31.5
23 Sugar	6.6	9.1	39.5	38
TOTAL	13.9	14.2		

Note: The average rank of the industries may be summarized as follows:

	Average Rank	
	1956	1966
Industries 1–20 (1956)	10.5	17.4
Industries 21–40 (1956)	30.5	23.6
All industries	20.5	20.5

Source: *First National City Bank Monthly Economic Letter*, April 1957 and 1958 and April 1967 and 1968.

Differential Biases in Accounting Rates of Return

An alternative hypothesis explaining the unexpected persistence of certain industries in high or low ranks has been offered: accounting rates of return may not be correlated with economic rates of return. There may be a persistent differential bias in the accounting in some industries. Accounting rates of return are generally biased upward because accounting principles are "conservative." That is, accountants usually charge to current expense intangible investments such as organization costs, costs of establishing trade connections and of breaking in equipment, expenditures on recruiting, selecting, and training personnel, outlays on promotion (including advertising), and outlays on research and development. All these activities produce future income and therefore create economic assets. But accountants do not record such "intangible" assets, with the result that the rate of return obtained by expressing income as a percentage of recorded assets is overstated because the cost of assets is understated.

For example, if a firm purchases a patent with a life of more than one year, that investment will usually be shown on the balance sheet as an asset. But if the firm carries on a research and development program, the outlays will be expensed even though valuable patents accrue as a result. Despite the fact that research and development outlays are the cost of acquiring these patents, they will be expensed, and the patents acquired by research and development investments will not be shown on the balance sheet. Yet a patent developed by the firm is just as valuable as an identical patent bought externally and the two are equally assets of the firm.

Any outlay that brings returns in future periods should be capitalized when we attempt to measure the relative attractiveness of various industries. Failure to capitalize the outlay misrepresents a firm's assets and current income and misrepresents the capital required to enter the industry and obtain the firm's income. Yet accountants cannot capitalize such outlays without violating generally accepted accounting principles. Since in some industries outlays on intangibles are large relative to outlays on physical assets and in others they are small, the failure to capitalize produces a substantial distortion of asset positions and net worth in those industries.

The greater measurement error in some industries could be a cause of a spurious persistence in a high rank. It is notable that the industries shown in Tables 1 and 2 as persisting at high ranks are those that make relatively large outlays on intangible assets—outlays that are expensed, with a resulting understatement of net worth greater than occurs in most industries. The pharmaceutical industry, the office equipment industry, and the instruments and photographic equipment group are all fairly research-intensive. The soap and cosmetics group is relatively promotion-intensive. Both research and promotion are usually expensed despite the fact that major portions of these outlays produce income in years later than those in which the outlays are made.[9] These outlays should be capitalized in the year they occur and charged against the revenues they produce in later years if the costs of obtaining those revenues are to be reported accurately.

Since charging these outlays to current expense distorts income as well as assets and net worth, it is not completely clear what net effect will be produced on the accounting rate of return. That rate of

---

[9] A list of studies demonstrating the long-lived effects of advertising can be found in Yale Brozen, "New FTC Policy from Obsolete Economic Doctrine," *Antitrust Law Journal*, vol. 41, no. 3 (1973), p. 484, note 27.

return may be biased upward or downward according to the size of current outlays for intangibles relative to past outlays.[10]

Professor Clarkson, in the present study, sets out to correct accounting rates of return in order to remove some of the differential effects of unrecorded intangible capital. Since the pharmaceutical industry has had persistently high accounting rates of return, he examines a pharmaceutical firm in detail, removing as much bias in its accounting as possible by taking account of its outlays on research and development and on promotion. Without correction for this source of bias, the average accounting return on book net worth in his firm is 17.3 percent over the 1965–1974 period. Correcting accounting income for the expensing of investment outlays and correcting net worth for the omission of intangible assets purchased by outlays on research and on promotion,[11] he arrives at a return of 11.1 percent on net worth—a decrease of 6.2 percentage points.[12]

Despite the decline in the rate of return of this pharmaceutical firm when corrected for outlays on intangible capital, it could still be possible that the drug industry would stay at its high rank among industries ranked by *corrected* rates of return. Firms in other industries might also show a decline in return on net worth if their research and promotion outlays were appropriately capitalized and depreciated, thus remaining in lower ranks. However, the pharmaceutical industry is our most research-intensive industry. One would ex-

---

[10] Robert Ayanian, taking advertising capital into account, found an increase in the adjusted rate of return over the accounting rate of return in one of the firms (H. J. Heinz) he analyzed in "Advertising and Rates of Return," *Journal of Law & Economics*, vol. 18, no. 2 (October 1975), p. 499.

[11] It has been argued that outlays on advertising create a barrier to entry, thus enabling firms to earn monopoly profits, and that capitalizing these expenses is no more legitimate than capitalizing monopoly profits for determining whether a competitive rate of return is being earned. The argument that advertising creates a barrier to entry hinges on its creating brand loyalty. However, Yale Brozen, "Is Advertising a Barrier to Entry?" *Advertising and Society* (New York: New York University Press, 1974), pp. 79-80, 90-93, argues that advertising is used to create disloyalty. F. R. Edwards, "More on Advertising and Competition in Banking," *The Antitrust Bulletin*, vol. 21, no. 1 (Spring 1976), produces evidence, in addition to that given in Brozen, confirming the thesis. J. M. Vernon, "Concentration, Promotion, and Market Share Stability in the Pharmaceutical Industry," *Journal of Industrial Economics*, vol. 19, no. 3 (July 1971), pp. 257-258, finds that brand loyalty in the pharmaceutical industry decreases with an increase in advertising and promotion.

[12] Even more striking results of taking intangible capital into account in computing rates of return for some firms have been found by Robert Ayanian, "Advertising and Rate of Return," p. 499, and by Harry Bloch, "Advertising and Profitability: A Reappraisal," *Journal of Political Economy*, vol. 82, no. 2, part 1, p. 285. See Tables C-1 and C-2 in Appendix C where these findings are discussed.

pect it to show a decline in corrected rate of return from accounting return greater than the decline in other industries.

Professor Clarkson recomputes return on net worth in eleven industries for which data are available. The corrected rate of return declines by a greater amount from the accounting return in the pharmaceutical industry than in any other industry. The average 1959–1973 corrected return in pharmaceuticals drops by 5.4 percentage points from the accounting return. The next largest drop for any industry, using the same correction procedure, is 3.2 percentage points in the electrical machinery industry (Table 16). The high profitability of the pharmaceutical industry turns out to be, in large part, an accounting illusion.

Other Factors Causing Differential Returns

Measurement error accounts for a major portion of the distance between the pharmaceutical industry's accounting rate of return and the all-industries' average return. Is the residual large enough to induce concern about the possible monopoly power in the industry? In Professor Clarkson's sample of firms and industries, uncorrected figures show the pharmaceutical industry return to be 7.1 percentage points above the average return earned. After removing the measurement error that results from inappropriate accounting for the two varieties of intangible capital, the distance is reduced to 3.3 percentage points (see Table 16).

Part of this remaining differential between the pharmaceutical rate of return and the average return in Clarkson's sample of industries is the consequence of some remaining measurement error. Other varieties of intangible capital—such as investment in the recruitment, selection, and training of a work force—remain unaccounted for. But this error is probably similar in most industries, although Professor Telser has demonstrated that concentrated industries invest disproportionately in human capital.[13] But the drug industry is not a concentrated industry.

There is a variety of promotional capital that is more heavily used in pharmaceuticals than in almost any other industry, and that may be an important source of relative distortion of accounting rates of return. Pharmaceutical firms spend as much on informing doctors of the results of their research—by means other than advertising— as they spend on research itself. Since data on the nonadvertising

---

[13] Lester Telser, *Competition, Collusion and Game Theory* (Chicago: Aldine-Atherton, 1972).

promotional outlays of other industries are scanty, it is not possible to determine the differential impact of these expenditures.

A second source of relative bias in drug industry figures is the risk factor. If risks are greater in the pharmaceutical arena than in most other industries, successful pharmaceutical firms will have a higher rate of return than successful firms in other industries.[14] (It is the profits of successful or "leading" firms in an industry that are used in the First National City Bank and FTC compilations of industry profit rates.)

There is reason to believe that pharmaceutical firms face greater risks even than those firms that explore for and produce crude oil, uranium, gold, copper, and other elusive minerals. The Pharmaceutical Manufacturers Association reported that its members "obtained, prepared, extracted or isolated" 126,000 compounds in 1970 and tested 704,000 compounds for pharmacological activity. Only 1,013 of these compounds proved promising and safe enough after testing in animals to move into clinical test.[15] Since fewer than twenty new compounds reach the market in a typical year,[16] this means that the investment in research and development produces an enormous number of "dry holes"—some of them very expensive—for every successful compound.[17] A firm may test thousands of compounds each year for many years and never hit a winner.[18] Those that do happen to hit a winner will appear to be very profitable while the industry may be relatively unprofitable. Since it is the firms with winners who survive and whose returns are measured to compute industry profitability, a biased figure is produced.

There are grounds for suspecting that the drug industry profit rates reported by the FTC, FNCB, and SEC, using a small number of firms and only the largest firms, overstate the industry's attractive-

---

[14] Richard Mancke, "Causes of Interfirm Profitability Differences: A New Interpretation of the Evidence," *Quarterly Journal of Economics*, vol. 88 (May 1974).

[15] Pharmaceutical Manufacturers Association, *Annual Survey Report, 1970-71*, p. 15.

[16] The number of new chemical entities marketed was sixteen in 1974 and twelve in 1975. The average annual number was fourteen from 1963 through 1975. Henry Grabowski, *Drug Regulation and Innovation* (Washington, D.C.: American Enterprise Institute for Public Policy Research, 1976), p. 18, Table 1.

[17] Merck & Co. "recently shelved a new drug for gout on which it had spent close to $20 million." Wyntham Robertson, "Merck Strains to Keep the Pots Aboiling," *Fortune*, vol. 93 (March 1976), p. 136.

[18] Merck has "in the last ten years, brought out only one commercially important drug in the U.S. market. . . . [D]uring this period the corporation has pumped almost $800 million into research." Robertson, "Merck Strains," pp. 134-135. "Since 1948, Merck has spent close to $90 million on antibiotics research without producing a . . . commercially successful product." Ibid., p. 168.

ness. From 1947 to 1967, the number of firms in the pharmaceutical preparations industry (SIC 2834) declined from 1,123 to 791.[19] If the industry were actually as profitable as reports from a small number of successful firms make it appear, the firms in the industry would find it attractive to remain and new firms would have been attracted to the industry. A declining number of firms is not usually found in an industry with true above-average returns or supracompetitive prices. Also, it is notable that the rate of decline in number of firms accelerated following the passage of the 1962 amendments to the Food, Drug, and Cosmetic Act, which increased the cost and riskiness of research[20] and contributed to a reduction in the expected rate of return on research from 11.4 percent in 1960 to 3.3 percent in 1973.[21]

A simple analogy may help to make it clear why the usual profitability figures reported for an industry such as the drug group and other relatively risky industries are biased upward relative to the profitability figures for less risky industries. The new entrant in petroleum exploration, if he has funds to finance the drilling of only one well, stands an 80 percent chance of going broke, assuming that one out of five wells represents the usual success ratio. If five firms enter the industry with such limited funds and the probability of success with any one well is one-fifth, four will fail and one will succeed. Assuming that each well costs $1,000, that the probability of success is one-fifth, and that the cost of capital is 10 percent, a successful well must promise a return of $500 in perpetuity[22] to

---

[19] U.S. Bureau of the Census, *Concentration Ratios in Manufacturing*, p. SR2-20.

[20] Martin N. Baily, "Research and Development Costs and Returns: The U.S. Pharmaceutical Industry," *Journal of Political Economy*, vol. 80, no. 1 (January/February 1972); Sam Peltzman, *Regulation of Pharmaceutical Innovation: The 1962 Amendments* (Washington, D.C.: American Enterprise Institute for Public Policy Research, 1974).

[21] David Schwartzman, *The Expected Return from Pharmaceutical Research* (Washington, D.C.: American Enterprise Institute for Public Policy Research, 1975), pp. 36, 44.

[22] We simplify the arithmetic of the discussion by using perpetual returns. A limited-life well's cash flow can be converted to the equivalent perpetuity and this discussion can be thought of as using perpetuities equivalent to the actual cash flows from a well. In terms of the example used here, a ten-year-life well yielding $500 in perpetuity, given a 10 percent cost of capital (yield on alternative investments), would be one, for instance, that yielded a $5,000 return of capital over the ten years (a uniform return of $500 of capital each year for ten years, for example) plus a uniformly declining income yield, declining from $500 the first year to $50 in the last year. The perpetual income stream of $500 is maintained by the investment of the recaptured capital in the alternative uses yielding 10 percent. This growing income stream from the alternative uses maintains a level total income stream of $500 when combined with the declining net income (after depletion) from the well.

attract investment to the exploration industry. That is, the average five-well drilling program will require a $5,000 investment and, with one well out of five *always* successful, a $500 annual return on that one well will yield a 10 percent return on the $5,000 investment and the industry can compete for capital. Each company investing $1,000 faces a one-fifth chance of making $500 a year. Each faces a probable return of $100 (one-fifth probability times $500).

With these five firms each drilling one well, four fail and one succeeds. The successful company will have invested $1,000, will earn $500 a year, and will show a 50 percent return on investment. It is this high return on the one successful well that attracts sufficient capital to our hypothetical oil exploration industry to provide a large number of producing wells. Only by drilling 500 wells can we get 100 producing wells. Capital will not be invested in drilling 500 wells unless the return on investment in successful wells is large enough to provide a probable yield of 10 percent to the investment in each well—dry or wet.

If 100 firms succeed among the 500 who try, the 100 successes will show an average 50 percent return. The industry will appear to be very profitable indeed. Only the successful firms will be reporting their income each year, the 400 failures having disappeared from the scene.

Does the 50 percent average return in firms producing crude oil mean that consumers are being victimized? Are resources being prevented from entering the industry by monopolists who are barring entry to the industry? Should controls be imposed on the price of oil to reduce returns to 10 percent in these 100 successful firms? If we do impose such controls, the return from a successful well will be reduced to $100 per year. The probable return to a drilling venture will drop to 2 percent (one-fifth probability of a $100 return or a $20 probable return on a $1000 investment). Drilling investment will cease in these circumstances. No further additions to the stock of producing wells will occur.

Of course, not all currently operating petroleum producers earn a uniformly high return. There are several reasons for this. One lies in the fact that successful wildcatters usually continue to wildcat. The one hundred successful firms, having been successful, will, let us assume, all drill a second well. Of these, one out of five succeeds again. Twenty firms will hit a second wet hole, will have two producing wells, and will continue to earn a 50 percent return. The remaining eighty will each have a $500 return from their successful wells but will now have invested $2,000, the second $1,000 having gone into a dry hole. Their return will drop to 25 percent. There are now twenty firms, which are the largest in the industry, earning a 50 percent rate of return and eighty smaller firms producing half as much and earning a 25 percent return.[23]

A third round of drilling will further increase the dispersion and will leave us with even larger firms earning the highest rate of return. Of the twenty largest, on the third round, four will succeed in drilling another wet hole. Four firms will be earning 50 percent on their investment in three successful wells. Sixteen of the former twenty largest will each be earning $1,000 on their $3,000 investment in two wet holes and one dry hole for a 33 percent return. Of the eighty firms with one producing well, sixteen (one-fifth of the eighty) will strike a second producing well and will also be earning 33 percent. But sixty-four will have drilled two dry holes and will be earning 17 percent. We can set out the results in tabular form.

Number of Firms	Number of Wet Holes per Firm	Return (percent)
4	3	50
32	2	33
64	1	17
400	firms no longer in existence	

Since current records show only the firms still in business, the industry will appear to be very profitable despite the fact that the probable return on investment to any new entrant is still 10 percent and the probable return on any additional wells drilled by currently operating firms is also only 10 percent. If all the firms go into a fourth round of drilling, each investing $1,000 in another well, the distribution shown in the table below will result:

Number of Firms	Number of Wet Holes per Firm	Return (percent)
1	4	50
9	3	38
39	2	25
51	1	13
400	firms no longer in existence	

[23] Harold Demsetz, in *The Market Concentration Doctrine* (Washington, D.C.: American Enterprise Institute for Public Policy Research, 1973), pp. 19-20, points out that industries may become concentrated with larger firms in those industries showing higher rates of return than smaller firms not only because of luck but also because of "socially desirable superior performance" of the larger firms.

Perhaps it might be argued that the one firm earning 50 percent should do no more drilling (research) since it has only a one-fifth chance of maintaining its 50 percent return. But it faces a probable return of 10 percent, the same return that induced it to drill in the first place. Presumably, this return is as attractive as it always was. This is the same chance it faced when it drilled its second, third, and fourth (and its first) wet hole. So let us assume that all firms go into a fifth round of drilling. The distribution shown below is the most likely result.

Number of Firms	Number of Wet Holes per Firm	Return (percent)
3	4	40
15	3	30
41	2	20
41	1	10
400	firms no longer in existence	

The surviving 100 firms have an above-average return as a group. The industry apparently is earning an average 18 percent return on the $500,000 invested in sinking 500 wells. The 180 producing wells, however, are the result of sinking 900 wells, 400 by firms that have long since disappeared. If we count the $400,000 investment of the defunct firms, the industry is earning only a 10 percent return on its *total* investment (and has always earned that return).[24] We have 180 producing wells only because each firm hoped to be one of the surviving 100—and, preferably, one of the big three with the four wet holes.

This is the situation we see in the pharmaceutical industry, except that the chances of a successful discovery (a wet hole) are slimmer for pharmaceutical firms than in the hypothetical oil industry postulated above, and the average cost of a successful discovery relative

[24] Given the actual accounting practices of crude-oil exploration and production firms, accounts of successful firms would have to be corrected (and capital invested by defunct firms taken into account) to arrive at the true return in crude oil. S. David Anderson, "Review of F. Allvine and J. M. Patterson, *Competition Ltd.*," *Yale Law Journal*, vol. 82 (1973), pp. 1355-1361; Shyam Sunder, "Properties of Accounting Numbers under Full Costing and Successful Efforts Costing in the Petroleum Industry," *The Accounting Review*, vol. 51, no. 1 (January 1976), pp. 1-18.

to the size of the total market is higher. The average cost of discovering and winning FDA acceptance of a new pharmaceutical chemical is in excess of $20 million.[25] To discover one such chemical, pharmaceutical research and development programs synthesize and test thousands of substances. Of these, a few are promising enough after animal tests to go to clinical trial. Out of these, very few safe and effective chemicals emerge, and perhaps none. Many of the new drugs that do emerge barely pay their production and marketing costs leaving little or nothing to provide any return on the investment in research and development. Some are successful enough to return at least some of the capital invested in research and development. A few are very successful and provide the bulk of a firm's return on its research and development investment.

In view of the large risks in drug industry research and development,[26] it is surprising that successful firms show as little premium as they do over the average rate of return in all industry.[27] No Henry Ford billionaires have emerged from the drug industry, and there are no firms reporting rates of return of 100 percent or more, as the Ford Motor Company did in its early days[28]—or of 58 to 76 percent, as Nash did in 1927–1929, or of 29 to 42 percent, as Hudson did in 1927–1929, or of 36 to 66 percent, as Packard did in 1927–1929.[29] Internal Revenue Service categorizations of corporate tax returns show a number of companies earning in excess of 100 percent

[25] David Schwartzman, *The Expected Return from Pharmaceutical Research*, p. 28.

[26] G. R. Conrad and I. H. Plotkin, "Risk/Return: U.S. Industry Pattern," *Harvard Business Review*, vol. 46, no. 2 (March-April 1968), p. 96, find the drugs and allied products industry to be the fourth-riskiest industry out of fifty-nine, using dispersions of book rates of return among firms in each industry as the measure of risk. This measure tends to understate an industry's relative riskiness where a large proportion of firms has disappeared and where each of the remaining successful firms has attempted a large number of projects with a resultant convergence of rates of return among the successful firms.

[27] The automobile industry also provides an example of a very risky industry, perhaps riskier than the pharmaceutical industry. Most firms have failed to survive and the few surviving firms show high rates of return. As a consequence of using only the rates of return of surviving firms to measure the industry rate of return, the automobile industry has appeared to be highly profitable. As the Federal Trade Commission has pointed out, however, "The profits of the motorcar manufacturers have varied greatly according to time and circumstance. The path of the industry's growth is strewn with scores of companies that have failed. . . ." *Report on Motor Vehicle Industry* (Washington, D.C.: U.S. Government Printing Office, 1940), p. 1061. The *Report* goes on to point out that, "For many years the automobile industry was regarded as highly speculative," p. 1063.

[28] Federal Trade Commission, *Report on Motor Vehicle Industry*, pp. 624, 634.

[29] Ibid., pp. 692, 709, 757.

on their assets,[30] but apparently none of these are to be found in the pharmaceutical industry. Competition in the industry must be very severe indeed to keep those firms which discover—or invent and develop—the largest selling products from earning really significant premiums from their fortunate experiences in the assumption of research and development risks.

Yale Brozen
Graduate School of Business
University of Chicago

---

[30] In 1957, 671 corporations exceeded this level. Average assets per firm were $11,200. U.S. Treasury Department, Internal Revenue Service, *Corporation Income Tax Returns*, July 1957-June 1958 (Washington, D.C.: U.S. Government Printing Office, 1960), p. 116.

INTRODUCTION

During the past ten years, rapidly rising prices have prompted increasingly careful inquiry into the relationships between prices and profits.[1] One occasional result of such investigations has been administrative or judicial action or the passage of legislation altering the rules regulating economic activity in industries with high reported rates of return. Some of the provisions of the Kefauver-Harris drug amendments of 1962 (Public Law 87-78), for example, resulted from the U.S. Senate's investigations of administered prices during the late 1950s and early 1960s. More recent examples include investigations of the oil and natural gas industry and the legislation empowering the Federal Energy Agency to regulate prices of petroleum products and crude oil. Inquiries and associated decisions by the President's Council on Wage and Price Stability and the antitrust agencies in the United States and by the National Board for Prices and Incomes and the Monopolies Commission in Great Britain—provide examples of activities by administrative agencies, based on views of the relationship between prices and profits and the meaning of various levels of profit.

Behind many administrative and legislative actions is the notion that price increases and high profits are directly related to barriers to entry or to anticompetitive practices.[2] There is, however, considerable

A number of useful comments and suggestions on an earlier draft were provided by Yale Brozen, Louis De Alessi, and Douglas L. Cocks.

[1] U.S. Congress, Senate, Subcommittee on Antitrust and Monopoly, Committee on the Judiciary, *Administered Prices: A Compendium on Public Policy*, 88th Cong., 1st sess., 1963, p. 3.

[2] See J. S. Bain, "The Profit Rate as a Measure of Monopoly Power," *Quarterly Journal of Economics*, vol. 55, no. 2 (February 1941), pp. 271-293; also E. Mansfield, "Industrial Research and Development: Characteristics, Costs, and Diffusion

evidence that such linkages do not exist [3] and that high or low accounting profit levels in some industries merely reflect disequilibrium forces, specific legislation (such as the Motor Transportation Act of 1935), risk, the failure to account for intangible capital (measurement error), or other natural or social forces.[4] If beliefs about such linkages are based on inaccurate information, the resulting legislative policies may produce serious misallocations of resources. If the reported high accounting profits of some industries produce hostile legislative or administrative action when the reports are the result of accounting-induced illusion (measurement error), the result may be to drive resources away from socially desirable uses.

The fact that high *economic* profits in an *industry* may be a result of monopoly power in that industry has caused confusion among antitrust agencies. They have reacted against high *accounting* profits in *firms*,[5] whether or not industry economic profits were high, in cases where the accounting rate of return may have been illusory or may have been a consequence of socially desirable efficiency in the firm. Often, firms' high economic profits are the consequence of actions that create efficiency and lead to prices lower than are charged by low-profit firms or would be charged in the absence of the high-profit firms.[6]

This study is concerned with expanding our knowledge of the relationships among intangible capital, rates of return, and investment. In the determination of these relationships, special attention is given to the nature of the industry (especially the nature of the pharma-

of Results," *Papers and Proceedings of the Eighty-First Annual Meeting of the American Economic Association, American Economic Review*, vol. 59, no. 2 (May 1969), pp. 65-71.

[3] See Steven Lustgarten, *Industrial Concentration and Inflation* (Washington, D.C.: American Enterprise Institute for Public Policy Research, 1975).

[4] Yale Brozen, "The Antitrust Task Force Deconcentration Recommendation," *Journal of Law and Economics*, vol. 13, no. 2 (October 1970), pp. 279-292; "Bain's Concentration and Rates of Return Revisited," *Journal of Law and Economics*, vol. 14, no. 2 (October 1971), pp. 351-370; "Barriers Facilitate Entry," *The Antitrust Bulletin*, vol. 14 (Winter 1969), pp. 851-854; Robert Ayanian, "Advertising and the Rate of Return," *Journal of Law and Economics*, vol. 18, no. 2 (October 1975); H. Bloch, "Advertising and Profitability: A Reappraisal," *Journal of Political Economy*, vol. 82, no. 2 (March/April 1974), pp. 267-286.

[5] See James C. Ellert, *Antitrust Enforcement and the Behavior of Stock Prices* (Chicago: University of Chicago Press, forthcoming).

[6] See John S. McGee, " 'Competition' and the Number of Firms," *In Defense of Industrial Concentration* (New York: Praeger Publishers, 1971), reprinted in Yale Brozen, ed., *The Competitive Economy: Selected Readings* (Morristown, N. J.: General Learning Press, 1975); and Sam Peltzman, "The Gains and Losses from Industrial Concentration," *Journal of Political Economy*, forthcoming.

ceutical industry),[7] the decision-making process, and the measurement of economic activities.

Chapter 1 of this study examines the differences between real and measured output and real and measured use of resources. Chapter 2 discusses difficulties in obtaining an unbiased measure of the returns to investment and the applicability of uncorrected accounting rate-of-return measurements. The accounting rate of return in drug firms has been recognized as being abnormally biased, and the industry has been singled out for special attention in a number of studies.[8] We single it out here also with a somewhat wider-than-usual cast of the net to capture the effects of intangible capital. Accounting data from a pharmaceutical firm with intangible capital unrecognized on accounting statements are used in Chapter 3 to correct rate-of-return measurements. Both research and development capital and promotion capital are incorporated in the analysis. Finally, Chapter 4 examines the consequences of correcting rate-of-return measurements in other industries as well as in the drug industry, and analyzes the way adjusting profits to take account of price changes affects high rate-of-return industries.

The findings of this study suggest that existing measures of profitability are significantly and differentially biased. The application of appropriate corrections to conventional accounting rates of return has substantial effects on the measured rate of return and on relative rates of return among industries. These findings indicate that even minor adjustments in eliminating the biases resulting from the expensing of advertising and research expenditures produce marked changes in measured rates of return in some industries.

Since these adjustments are consistent with economic theory and reflect determinants of managerial choices, corrected returns rather

---

[7] Some of these relationships in the pharmaceutical industry have been analyzed in previous studies. See, for example, Martin Baily, "Research and Development Costs and Return: The U.S. Pharmaceutical Industry," *Journal of Political Economy*, vol. 80, no. 1 (January/February 1972), pp. 70-85; Robert B. Helms, ed., *Drug Development and Marketing* (Washington, D.C.: American Enterprise Institute for Public Policy Research, 1975); David Schwartzman, *The Expected Return on Investment in Pharmaceutical Research* (Washington, D.C.: American Enterprise Institute, 1975); Rodney Smith, "Ethical Drug Industry Return on Investment" (Ph.D. diss., University of Massachusetts, 1974); and Thomas Stauffer, "The Measurement of Corporate Rate of Return: A Generalized Formulation," *Bell Journal of Economics and Management Science*, vol. 2, no. 2 (Autumn 1971), pp. 434-469.

[8] Robert Ayanian, "Profit Rates and Economic Performance of Drug Firms," in *Drug Development and Marketing*; and Jesse J. Friedman and Murray N. Friedman, "Relative Profitability and Monopoly Power," *Conference Board Record*, December 1972, pp. 49-58.

than unadjusted accounting returns are appropriate for public inquiries. Furthermore, since the application of these corrections decreases major differentials among the returns of firms and industries, it is evident that the monopoly explanation of firm behavior has been overemphasized in congressional hearings and economic literature. More attention should be given to obtaining economically sound measurements of profit rates in each firm and industry. At this point—on the basis of the information assembled here—it seems likely that the traditional reasons given for differences in rates of return among industries where prices and entry are not regulated (entry barriers, concentration) do not produce major rate-of-return differentials. Observed differences in profitability seem to be for the most part the consequence of systematic (and correctable) measurement errors.

1
ECONOMIC AND ACCOUNTING MEASURES

> The unadjusted accounting rate of profit, as computed by the usual methods from balance sheets and income statements, is *prima facie* an absolutely unreliable indicator of the presence or absence either of monopoly power or of excess profits. . . . The relationship between price and accounting average cost tells us nothing about the degree of monopoly power, and little about the extent of excess profit.[1]

For the most part, investigations of the structure and performance of firms and industries have been aimed at identifying the real relationships among output, resource use, and relative prices. In these investigations the analyst should be indifferent between income statements expressed in Deutschemarks or dollars, as long as the yardstick used does not vary in size over time. But accounting statements are expressed in "rubbery" value units—units that expand and contract. This prevents them from being directly useful for understanding whether a firm or industry is becoming more or less profitable than it has been. Nominal profits and accounting rates of return rose in 1974, for example, yet real profits declined.[2] Plans to expand capacity were curtailed, and the stock market fell in both real and nominal terms despite the increase in accounting rates of return.

Expansion (including entry) and contraction (including exit) choices by decision makers will not depend, for example, on whether the firm uses LIFO or FIFO to measure cost of goods sold and

---

[1] Bain, "The Profit Rate," p. 291.
[2] George Terborgh, *Inflation and Profits* (Washington, D.C.: Machinery and Allied Products Institute, 1976).

inventory values.[3] Nor do they depend on whether accounting rates of return shown by firms or industries are high or low. Investors try to look at real relationships rather than at accounting figures.[4] Any serious study of industrial organization and resource allocation must, therefore, be concerned with real measures of economic activity. After all, if a financial unit of account were a fixed measure of real value, Congress could make everyone rich by increasing the money supply tenfold.

Accurate measurement of the real use of resources, however, is costly: consider, for example, a firm's decision to expand capacity and increase output. This decision requires a measure of the prospective economic return on the additional investment in capacity. Unfortunately, the accounting rate of return provides a poor measure of the economic rate of return even on investment currently in place, thereby negating its usefulness as an index to the potential return on additional investment or on maintenance of current capacity. Even its value for regulatory purposes has been seriously questioned. For example, the Louisiana Public Service Commission, in a 1976 opinion, said:

> South Central Bell expenses . . . a substantial amount of cost which was incurred for research and fundamental development (R&D).
>
> We feel that while this treatment of research and development costs may be an acceptable accounting treatment it is not an appropriate treatment of research and development costs for the determination of proper rates.
>
> Reflection on the nature of research and development effort will show that it is an improper rate making treatment to currently expense the cost associated with research and development. By definition, research and development effort is undertaken to find new or improved processes or products and new facts which will enhance the future welfare of South Central Bell. There is no difference between research and development costs and any other costs which will benefit future ratepayers. Thus, just as other costs which benefit future ratepayers are capitalized and expensed in the future, so should research and development costs.

[3] Since this choice could influence current tax liabilities—on which see William Fellner, Kenneth Clarkson and John H. Moore, *Correcting Taxes for Inflation* (Washington, D.C.: American Enterprise Institute for Public Policy Research, 1975)—the firm may not be indifferent to these methods. However, long-run expansion or contraction will generally not depend on the alternative chosen.

[4] Charles R. Nelson, "Inflation, Taxes, and the Value of Corporate Shares," *Proceedings*, Center for Research in Security Prices (Chicago: Graduate School of Business, University of Chicago, 1974).

The fact that accountants often treat research and development expenditures as a current expense is no reason for doing so for regulatory purposes. It appears that the basic reason why accountants reflect research and development as a current expense is that there is uncertainty or at minimum, a high degree of risk associated with the prediction of the future revenue accomplishments associated with research and development costs as compared to other asset expenditures. When faced with a high degree of uncertainty, the accountant invokes the convention of conservation and effects an immediate charge off of research and development costs. This conservative approach is, however, in conflict with the more basic underlying accounting concept which calls for an association of costs with the time periods benefited and/or the revenues produced by such costs.

In order to bring South Central Bell's net operating income into accord with sound principles of regulation and economics, we have made an adjustment to reflect the capitalization and subsequent amortization of research and development costs. . . . After allowing for annual amortization at the overall depreciation rate of 5.3% and a return of 13.33% (the allowed before-tax rate of return in 1975) on the capitalized portion of research and development, we find that an after tax adjustment to increase net operating income of $853,000 is required.[5]

Current Value, Time, and Intangible Capital Adjustments

To determine whether a firm or industry is earning returns in excess of the competitive equilibrium rate—that is, in excess of what the capital invested would earn in the best alternative use to which it might be put—one must know the relationship of net revenues to the investment that would be required to duplicate existing capacity at present prices. Also, one must know how that relationship (which is the firm's rate of return) compares with the average economic rate of return in other industries. The capital required to duplicate capacity now in place in a firm is seldom shown on the ordinary balance sheet.[6]

[5] Louisiana Public Service Commission, *Opinion*, June 15, 1976, Docket Number U-12785.

[6] Plans are under way to require firms to present current value figures as well as historic figures. Objections have been raised, however, because this would increase accounting costs in the typical firm by something on the order of 10 percent. See Adolf J. Enthoven, "Replacement-value accounting: wave of the

Usually, instead, the historical costs of acquisition of assets are shown. But after a period of inflation, historical costs grossly understate the current or market value of the assets and the cost of replacement.[7] In addition, most balance sheets omit the intangible capital that has been invested in the business—such investment as the cost of establishing trade connections, organizing and training a work force, and outlays on research and development. Although these outlays are usually charged off as current expenses, they should, to make economic sense, be categorized as investments. They are investments because they produce income in future years and, moreover, they are frequently made at times when they add little or nothing to current income.

In industries where intangible investments are required, no firm will enter the industry if it can expect to earn only enough to provide what appears to be the competitive return on physical assets and working capital alone. The *pro forma* accounting rate of return on physical assets and working capital normally will be high in such industries since it includes the income from the complementary (intangible) capital that must be used in production if the physical assets are to earn a competitive rate of return.

The inappropriateness of historical costs for measuring the asset base of an industry can be illustrated by a familiar example from the housing industry. Suppose apartments built in 1957 cost $10,000 each and have a forty-year "life," that depreciation is charged on a straight-line basis, and that the apartments currently (1977) earn $1,800 each annually, after all costs other than depreciation and capital costs. If we subtract $250 depreciation ($10,000 divided by the forty years of "life"), the net return for 1977 is $1,550 on a $5,000 depreciated cost ($10,000 original "cost" less twenty years' depreciation at $250 per year). Apartments built for occupancy in 1957 would therefore appear to be earning a 31 percent return in 1977.

Does this indicate that entry is barred or that barriers to entry are high? Is this accounting rate of return excessive and an indication of the presence of monopoly? Actually, neither is the case. This accounting rate of return is an overstatement of the current rate of return. If construction costs in nominal or current terms have doubled

future?" *Harvard Business Review*, vol. 54, no. 1 (January-February 1976), pp. 6-8; Robert Mims, "More realism in inflation accounting," *Business Week*, January 19, 1976, p. 26; and Joseph M. Burns, *Accounting Standards and International Finance: With Special Reference to Multinationals* (Washington, D.C.: American Enterprise Institute for Public Policy Research, 1976).

[7] See Fellner, Clarkson, and Moore, *Correcting Taxes for Inflation*.

since the apartments were built, increasing the nominal capital required to duplicate an apartment to $20,000, then the $250 depreciation charge is an understatement and net income is overstated. Since replacement cost (new) has increased to $20,000, the depreciation rate at current market values is $500. Net income, therefore, is only $1,300, not $1,550. If the measuring unit for value, dollars, has been cut in half, the asset should be valued at $10,000 in 1977 dollars instead of $5,000 in 1957 dollars. The current value-adjusted accounting rate of return is 13 percent, not 31 percent.

But after these adjustments have been made, the currently stated rate of return does not give us a measure of the yield on the investment. If the apartment were duplicated new at a cost of $20,000, the net return of $1,300 would appear to yield 6.5 percent. This, too, is inaccurate. With no further inflation, the accounting rate-of-return figure becomes 13 percent in the twentieth year of the apartment's life and 26 percent in the thirtieth year. The true (or time-adjusted) yield on the investment over its life is approximately 10 percent, despite the fact that accounting rates of return rise from 6.5 percent in the first year to 26 percent in the thirtieth year and even higher in later years.

This exemplifies the meaninglessness of the accounting rate of return unadjusted for inflation or for time. Anyone currently considering investment in constructing and operating apartments cannot rely on *pro forma* accounting rates of return from the income statements and balance sheets of today's apartment operators. Biases in accounting rates of return reported by currently operating firms make these figures unreliable as a guide in determining whether an industry is worth entering or even whether rates of return are relatively high or low.

Suppose, for example, a pharmaceutical firm with assets of $100 million earns $30 million before research and development expenditures and spends $29 million on research and development, leaving an accounting income of $1 million. Does this 1 percent accounting rate of return mean that the investment of $100 million in net assets should not have been made?

If the firm spends $29 million in the current year on research and promotion, and this outlay is all for the purpose of producing revenues in future years, it should all be capitalized instead of being treated as an expense. In that case, the *pro forma* accounting rate of return would appear to be 30 percent. However, if we capitalize current research and promotion, we should capitalize past research and promotion and their capitalized value should appear on the balance sheet. Similarly, a depreciation charge on this intangible capital should appear in the income statement. If the net research and promotion (intangible) capital of the firm amounts to $100 million in the current year and the depreciation of that capital amounts to $10 million, then the assets of the firm amount to $200 million and current income is $20 million ($100 million book value plus $100 million intangible capital, and $30 million gross income less $10 million depreciation). The adjusted rate of return must be 10 percent instead of 1 percent.

This discussion suggests the reasons that accounting data do not provide useful economic measures. Of course, if all accounting rates of return contained proportionate biases, then rates could still be useful for comparing industries: we could still use them to determine whether any industries are persistently more or less profitable than the average. But they do not. Those industries which have invested relatively more in intangible capital, or whose physical assets are concentrated more heavily than the average in older age brackets, will show accounting rates of return biased upward when compared to those of other industries.

Use of Alternative Measurements

The inappropriateness of standard accounting measurements for investment decisions does not, however, imply that accounting measurements have no value. One of the distinguishing characteristics of a firm (or any economic organization) is the suppression of the price mechanism in most exchange and production decisions within the enterprise.[8] Because much of the information about prices, quantities and qualities of resources, and outputs is not available in standard accounting statements, owners and managers of organizations create information systems for their internal evaluation, control, and decision-making activities. Managers of organizations therefore have internal information systems for controlling or monitoring economic activities —such as accounts to measure the use of materials, personnel, and related inputs. Other accounts (such as internally used profit or loss statements, for example) have been developed to provide information on the current profitability or cost position of the enterprise or its

[8] See Ronald Coase, "The Nature of the Firm," *Economica*, vol. 4 (November 1937), pp. 386-405, and Armen Alchian and Harold Demsetz, "Production, Information Costs, and Economic Organization," *American Economic Review*, vol. 62, no. 5 (December 1972), pp. 777-795, for a discussion of the rationale for and gains from organization within a firm.

parts. Still other measures (such as the special accounts and measurements required by the Internal Revenue Service) may be used to provide information required by law.

In general, the information provided by one type of account is usually too specific to be useful beyond its original purpose. For example, a divisional profit or loss statement will often give incorrect information for decisions involving the expansion or curtailment of operations in the short run. The reason for this lies in the fact that most profit and loss statements include fixed costs (both amortized acquisition and possession costs) as well as operating costs. An increase in a division's operations in the short run will contribute to profits as long as increased revenues are greater than incremental or increased out-of-pocket costs.[9] When incremental revenues are greater than incremental costs, both the division's profits and the firm's overall profits would be increased by expanding the operations of this division even when fixed or common costs are not covered. As the phrase goes, it is "contribution to overhead and profit" that is relevant. On the other hand, the information useful for short-run decisions does not provide the necessary basis for long-run exit and entry decisions for each of the divisions of the organization. Nor does it provide information for temporary shut-down decisions.

The use of a variety of measures for output and resources is not, of course, limited to profit-seeking enterprises. The U.S. government, for example, uses program accounts at the division or bureau level when it measures activities or outputs and uses object accounts to meter actual use of inputs.[10] U.S. aggregated accounts also differ according to the variety of information sought by the administration, Congress, and other interested parties. During the past fifteen years the administrative cash budget, consolidated cash budget, unified budget, and national income account budget have all been used in the U.S. budget and in the President's annual budget message to Congress. Each of these budget accounts provides a different measurement of total U.S. government activity.

Although different accounts or measurements are useful for different varieties of decision making and for monitoring a firm's activities, existing practices often negate much of the potential benefit from any particular measurement. For example, recent estimates indicate that there can be as many as 30 million different measures

---

[9] See "Airline Takes the Marginal Route," *Business Week*, April 20, 1963, for the classic application of this concept.

[10] See *The Budget of the U.S. Government, 1977*, Appendix, for examples of these accounts.

of net income using alternative (but acceptable) accounting procedures for recording inventory, depreciation, life cycle, and a firm's various transactions.[11] In the U.S. government, budgets of agencies that rent certain types of real property are higher for a given level of activity than those that own the same property because the budgets of the latter agencies do not include implicit costs of the services from previously acquired real property.[12] In such cases, direct comparisons of the costs of operations for these agencies yield biased outcomes.

Information for Investment Decisions

In determining the appropriate method for measuring the relationship between resources committed by and outputs resulting from investment decisions, we should give particular attention to those factors most likely to alter the returns from investment. These factors include but are not limited to (1) the period of resource accumulation before production begins, (2) the economic life of the resources after production begins, (3) the opportunity cost of the resources, (4) any changes in both absolute and relative price levels, (5) risk (however defined), and (6) the appropriability of rewards.

Because it may take anywhere from less than a year to three or four years before new plants begin production, and much longer before many research projects begin to pay off—the period of accumulation of capital before output is created is extremely important in measuring the comparative profitability of investment alternatives. And, of course, once in production, the resources have a finite economic life. When the two periods of accumulation of capital and economic life are combined, they define the economic life cycle of the investment project.

Moreover, since resources used in any project represent alternatives foregone in other possible projects, there is an "opportunity cost" of using resources in any investment. With the average after-tax rate of return as a base, the opportunity cost for capital is esti-

---

[11] R. J. Chambers, "A Matter of Principle," *Accounting Review*, vol. 41, no. 3 (July 1966), pp. 443-457, and Paul Grady, "Inventory of Generally Accepted Accounting Principles in the United States of America," *Accounting Review*, vol. 40, no. 1 (January 1965), pp. 21-30.

[12] Charles Schultze, "The Role of Incentives, Penalties, and Rewards in Attaining Effective Policy," in *The Analysis and Evaluation of Public Expenditures: The PPB System* (Washington, D.C.: U.S. Government Printing Office, 1969), vol. 1, and Kenneth Clarkson, "The Right Way, the Wrong Way and the Government Way," *Res Publica*, vol. 2, no. 4 (Fall 1974), pp. 14-19.

mated to be 10 percent per year.[13] This is the prescribed rate for U.S. government decisions on deferred costs and benefits.[14] In addition, since changes in relative and absolute prices will alter the net returns from investment projects, corrections for price level changes in the measures used must be made to prevent systematic biases in these measurements. Equally important, each investment must be weighted by its corresponding risk (or a risk premium must be subtracted from the present value of the investment).[15] Without such weighting, riskier projects would appear to yield higher returns than less risky alternatives (or have a positive present value when they actually have a negative value). Finally, all measurements must be corrected for the appropriability of returns to the enterprise. When an enterprise's net rewards or benefits are not capturable, the returns to the organization must be corrected accordingly for decision-making purposes. Under current income tax regulation, for example, corporate enterprises can be expected to receive approximately half of the net returns (defined under current accounting procedures) from any investment if the enterprise is financed by equity capital.

For decision-making purposes, the above relationships can be summarized in the following expression:[16]

$$PV = -\sum_{t=0}^{i-1} \frac{K_t(P_t)}{(1+r)^t} + \sum_{t+i}^{n} \frac{p(R_t - C_t)\,(P_t)}{(1+r)^t}\,(A_t) \qquad [1]$$

where PV = Present value of an investment
t = Year
K_t = Capital expenditures in year t
P_t = Price index for year t
r = Opportunity cost of capital
R_t = Gross revenues in year t
C_t = Manufacturing costs in year t
p = Probability of positive or favorable occurrence
A_t = Appropriability of returns to enterprise
i = Number of years before sales begin
n = End of the economic life for the investment

[13] See J. A. Stockfisch, "The Interest Rate Applicable to Government Investment Projects," in Harley Hinrichs and Graeme Taylor, eds., *Program Budgeting and Benefit-Cost Analysis* (Pacific Palisades, Calif.: Goodyear Publishing Co., 1969), pp. 187-201.
[14] *Discount Rates To Be Used in Evaluating Time-Distributed Costs and Benefits,* Office of Management and Budget, Circular A-94, March 27, 1972. This is the rate to be used after all inflation adjustments have been made.
[15] Harold Bierman and Seymour Smidt, *The Capital Budgeting Decision* (New York: The Macmillan Company, 1966), pp. 322-325.
[16] See Thomas Stauffer, "Profitability Measures in the Pharmaceutical Industry," in Helms, *Drug Development and Marketing*, pp. 97-119.

Thus, if the accumulated capital (corrected for changes in the price level and for the opportunity cost of capital) is less than expected discounted net revenues (corrected for changes in the price level and for appropriability factors), the present value of the investment will be positive and a wealth-maximizing enterprise would undertake the project.

Any modification of the parameters in [1] will alter the present value calculations. For example, if the probability of a favorable occurrence increases (p rises in [1]), then the present value of that investment will rise. On the other hand, if the appropriability of rewards falls (A_t decreases in [1]), then the present value declines and the investment will be curtailed or omitted.

2
RATE-OF-RETURN
MEASUREMENTS

Whenever the estimated present value (PV in expression [1]) of a project is greater than zero, investment in the project promises to be profitable and entrepreneurs or firms are motivated to undertake it. Actual returns will, of course, rarely match the predicted returns unless there are no risks (that is, by commonly accepted definitions, unless all future conditions are known with certainty). Nevertheless, explicit estimates of future returns are useful decision-making guidelines for new investment, expansion or shut-down plans, and exit or entry commitments. Estimated returns are also used by existing and potential stockholders for investment decisions and by elected officials for public policy decisions.

What is attempted here, however, is not an analysis of the prospective return in investment projects—what is known among economists as *ex ante* measurement. Instead, we are attempting to determine the rate of return on investments already made—what is known as *ex post* measurement. This is the purpose for which accounting rates of return have been used in various studies in spite of explicit recognition by some investigators that they are often poor proxies for the true rate of return.[1] Nevertheless, they have been accepted and used as proxies for the true rate of return for lack of better data, in studies of the relationships between and among concentration, advertising, and profits. Inferences which have been drawn from these studies for the making of public policy may or may not be correct— and the resulting public policies may be doing the nation a disservice if they are incorrect.

---

[1] Bain, "The Profit Rate."

Difficulties in Retrospective Measurements

Since information is not free and sometimes not available, measurement of the return from a project is plagued with serious problems. First, an enterprise rarely invests in a single project or completes one before starting additional ventures. As a consequence, one can neither simply examine the cash outflows of an enterprise before production to measure the capital invested in a project nor simply examine the cash inflows after production to measure net returns. Instead, one is faced with the difficult problem of identifying the outflows and inflows of numerous individual projects. When two or more projects begin at the same time, or cash inflow periods of the two overlap, identification becomes yet more difficult.

More important, enterprises with two or more projects will find that the lowest-cost production technique involves pooling assets and resources from different projects. Under such conditions, it is impossible to allocate the costs attributable to each project. In this joint-cost situation, even with no additional measurement problems, determination of the rate of return can be carried out only at the company level or at the division level where full cost separability by division is possible. Nonseparability of data also precludes measurement of the economic life cycle of each investment so that one must use some average of the returns for all projects over some average economic life.

The measured return at any point in time is likely to overestimate or underestimate the organization's actual rate of return. When measurement errors are not present, an estimate is still subject to all disequilibrium forces. For example, the measurement may be made during a general increase in the demand for the industry's products, but before entry by new (or expansion by existing) firms has been completed, so that there is a temporarily high return. This problem can be partly overcome by an examination of returns over several periods.

Finally, estimated returns are subject to measurement errors. With positive information and transaction costs, many of these cannot be eliminated—although certain errors, such as those discussed below, can be reduced. In such cases, it is important to make appropriate corrections.

Two generally used rate-of-return measurements are the ratio of current income from all projects to the current asset position of the firm and the ratio of that income to the equity position of the firm. These measurements reflect the difficulties discussed above as well as the relative ease of obtaining current income statistics from profit and loss statements and of obtaining asset or equity statistics from balance sheets. Unfortunately, there are several distortions in these conventional rate-of-return measurements—distortions that introduce systematic biases in the calculation. Some of these are, however, capable of correction.[2] The single most important bias in periods of moderate to low inflation is the practice of expensing advertising, promotion, and research and development outlays.[3] Other biases include (but are not limited to) the use of improper time dimensions and the failure to account for inflation or deflation.

Since these biases in the conventional accounting rate-of-return measurements can be corrected, there are strong reasons for modifying existing practices to produce more accurate measures of a firm's economic performance when comparisons are made among firms and industries. First, by identifying those resource expenditures that occur before actual production and by determining the appropriate economic life after production begins, we can significantly reduce the biases from expensing. Second, by measuring the rate of return over the life cycle of the chosen investments we can avoid biases such as those resulting from the omission of acquisition costs or fixed costs: this omission occurs when a period shorter than the life cycle is chosen and individual projects cannot be identified. Third, when rates of return compare cash inflows from investment in one period to cash outflows in another period, price adjustments must be made for changes in absolute and relative prices.

An examination of the factors determining present values for investment decisions and the procedure described above for estimating rates of return will show that some biases are capable of correction and can be eliminated in retrospective determinations of the rate of return earned by an enterprise. Adjustments required in estimating prospective returns—such as those for the probability of a favorable

---

[2] Many of these distortions have been known for some time. See, for example, O. Ladelle, "The Calculation of Depreciation," *The Accountant*, vol. 17 (November 1890), and Irving Fisher, *The Nature of Capital and Income* (1906; reprint ed., New York: Augustus M. Kelley, 1965).

[3] The bias involved in expensing advertising, research, and development costs has been recognized by many, including the Federal Trade Commission, "Annual Line of Business Report Program: Statement of Purpose," 1973; Friedman and Friedman, "Relative Profitability and Monopoly Power"; Ezra Solomon, "Alternative Rate of Return Concepts and Their Implications for Utility Regulation," *Bell Journal of Economic and Management Science*, vol. 1 (Spring 1970), pp. 65-81; Thomas Stauffer, "Measurement of Corporate Rates of Return"; and David Schwartzman, "Pharmaceutical R&D Expenditures and Rates of Return," Ayanian, "Profit Rates and Economic Performance," Stauffer, "Profitability Measures" in Helms, *Drug Development and Marketing*.

occurrence and for the appropriability of rewards [4]—are not necessary when estimating rates retrospectively. But other adjustments can be made—including those for price level changes and for intertemporal distribution of costs taking into account the total economic life cycle.

Even with these adjustments, not all the biases will be eliminated, and some new ones may be introduced. For example, in adjusting for both accumulation and depreciation, we must identify the resources to be included. Furthermore, we must find the appropriate total economic life of each resource identified. In addition, separating capital expenditures from current expenses during any period is not easy. Like data errors, not all of these problems can be eliminated. But even minimal adjustments (with some remaining potential corrections) yield significantly improved (that is, less biased) estimates of the true rate of return.

Basic Corrections in Accounting Rates of Return

The importance of correcting the accounting rate of return can be seen by comparing the conventional accounting with the corrected financial or economic rate of return for a hypothetical intangible-capital-intensive firm. Sales, current expenses, capital expenses for advertising and research, taxes, original profit, original net worth, and calculated rates of return on net worth for five years are shown for this hypothetical firm in the upper portion of Table 3. When advertising and research are currently expensed, the accounting rates of return are 8.0, 8.0, 13.0, 15.0, and 17.0 for the five years. If advertising expenditures yield revenues for three years and research expenditures accumulate for two years before they yield revenues for five years, the economic rates of return on net worth are 13.9, 12.5, 14.1, 14.0, and 13.4 percent for those years.

In the first year, corrected profits rise $8 million above the original *pro forma* profit of $8 million. Since only $2 million depreciation of the $6 million advertising expenditures and none of the $10 million research outlays are deducted in the first year, pretax profits are adjusted upwards by $14 million. If the tax rate is 50 percent, corrected profits increase by $7 million. In addition, the firm has unrealized (hence nontaxable) earnings of $1 million (10 percent of the $10 million research capital expenditure), representing the implicit

---

[4] The probability of expected net revenues when measuring prospective returns is shown as "p" in expression [1]. The appropriability of rewards is shown as "A_t."

Table 3
COMPARISON OF RATES OF RETURN FOR A HYPOTHETICAL FIRM UNDER ALTERNATE ACCOUNTING SYSTEMS
(amounts in millions of 1973 dollars)

Conventional Accounting Rates of Return

Year	Sales	Current expenses	Advertising	Research	Pretax profit	Taxes	Aftertax profit	Net worth	Rate of return on net worth
1	100.0	68.0	6.0	10.0	16.0	8.0	8.0	100.0	8.0%
2	100.0	68.0	6.0	10.0	16.0	8.0	8.0	100.0	8.0
3	120.0	75.0	9.0	10.0	26.0	13.0	13.0	100.0	13.0
4	130.0	78.0	12.0	10.0	30.0	15.0	15.0	100.0	15.0
5	140.0	84.0	12.0	10.0	34.0	17.0	17.0	100.0	17.0

Economic Rates of Return

Year	Sales less current expenses	Advertising depreciation	Net advertising capital a	Research depreciation b	Net research capital c	Corrected aftertax profits d	Corrected net worth	Corrected rate of return on net worth
1	32.0	2.0	4.0	0.00	11.00	16.00	115.00	13.9%
2	32.0	4.0	6.0	0.00	23.10	16.10	129.10	12.5
3	45.0	7.0	8.0	2.42	32.78	19.89	140.78	14.1
4	52.0	9.0	11.0	4.84	40.04	21.18	151.04	14.0
5	56.0	11.0	12.0	7.26	44.88	20.97	156.88	13.4

a Advertising and promotion are depreciated for three years.
b Research depreciates for five years.
c Research accumulates for two years at 10 percent.
d Increases in profits are taxed at 50 percent except for unrealized 10 percent earnings of incomplete research projects.
Source: See calculations in text.

flow of returns from research and development expenditures.[5] Because these returns are not taxed under existing federal regulations, the full correction for profits is $8 million (50 percent of $14 million plus $1 million). At the same time, net worth rises by $15 million ($4 million from the balance of advertising expenditures and $11 million from the accumulation of $10 million research expenditure at 10 percent).

In the second year, corrected aftertax profits rise by $8.1 million and net worth by $29.1 million ($2 million from the balance of first-year advertising expenditures, $4 million from the second-year balance of expenditures, $12.1 million from the second-year accumulation of first-year research expenditures, and $11 million from the accumulated research expenditures in the second year).

In the third year, the first-year research expenditures (which have become an asset) start yielding increased revenues. Depreciation of this asset begins in that year. During this year, corrected profits rise by $6.89 million ($9 million advertising outlays less $7 million advertising depreciation), which gives $2 million, times 0.5 for the 50 percent tax rate, which gives $1 million, plus the net of $10 million research outlays less $2.42 million research depreciation, which is $7.58 million and which is multiplied by the same 0.5 to give $3.79 million plus 21 million multiplied by 0.1 (nontaxable earnings for one year's research accumulation of $10 million and two years' research accumulation of $10 million at 10 percent), which gives $2.1 million—the three being added together for the $6.89 million. Corrected net worth rises to $140.78 million. The $40.78 million increase is composed of $2 million from the balance of advertising expenditures in the second year, $6 million from the balance of advertising expenditures in the third year, $9.68 million ($12.1 less $2.42 equalling $9.68) from the balance of research capital in the third year, $12.1 million from accumulation of research expenditures from the second year, and $11 million from accumulation of research expenditures in the third year.

Corrected profits and net worth for subsequent periods may be found by solving

---

[5] Previous rate-of-return studies have not included unrealized income from (nor increased capitalization of) expenditures whose returns begin at some future period. On the other hand, the inclusion of interest capitalized on plant construction work (an asset whose returns begin in the future) as operating income in computing earned rate of return (when plant construction is included in the rate base) is commonly practiced by public utilities and accepted by public utility commissions. See, for example, Public Utilities Commission, State of Connecticut, Docket No. 11601, 1974, p. 10.

$$CP = OP + (AE - DA)(1 - TR)$$
$$\qquad + (RE - DR)(1 - TR) + (AR)(r) \qquad [2]$$
$$CW = OW + BE + BR + AR \qquad\qquad\qquad [3]$$

where CP = Corrected profits
OP = Original profits
AE = Current advertising expenditures
DA = Depreciation of current and past advertising expenditures
RE = Current research expenditures
DR = Depreciation of past research expenditures
AR = Accumulated research expenditures
TR = Marginal tax rate
r = Opportunity cost of capital
CW = Corrected net worth
OW = Original net worth
BE = Balance of undepreciated advertising expenditures
BR = Balance of undepreciated research expenditures

For the above example, the solutions to [2] and [3] for the fourth and fifth year are given in Table 3.

The results show that these corrections may make significant differences in the rate of return. For example, the conventional accounting rate of return for the fifth year in this example is 17 percent, while the economic rate of return is 13 percent. Furthermore, if transition years are omitted (necessary when previous advertising-promotion and research capital stocks are unknown), the average rate of return falls. In this example the average conventional rate of return is 15.0 percent and the average economic rate of return is 13.8 percent for years three through five.[6] More important, the variance around the average rate of return falls significantly (from .03 to .001) when these corrections are applied to the original accounting data. This is particularly important when one recognizes that the real activities of the firm in this example are relatively constant in each of the five years.

Of course, differences between accounting and economic measurements are a function of several variables—including (1) the amount and growth rate of intangible capital outlays, (2) the lag in and length of the research and development cycle, (3) the opportunity cost of capital, and (4) the economic depreciation of capital expendi-

---

[6] Both unweighted and weighted (by net worth) rates of return are 15.0 and 13.8 percent for the conventional and economic three-year average.

tures—but the general conclusion holds. Corrected rates of return (and associated variances) will differ from the accounting rates of return. In most cases, accounting rates of return are biased upwards when capital activities have been expensed.

3
PHARMACEUTICAL
MANUFACTURING:
AN APPLICATION

The use of the appropriate price level adjustments, capital outlay levels, and capital accumulation and depreciation periods is relatively straightforward once the data are in hand. Unfortunately, except for price level adjustments, the data are elusive; conventional accounting procedures do not make it possible for us to identify all the transactions that should be included as capital outlays nor do they make it possible for us to determine accumulation and depreciation periods. Let us consider one industry—pharmaceuticals—as an example.

In the pharmaceutical industry a fraction of capital outlays incurred for manufacturing plants (and some other capital outlays) are capitalized and depreciated. For some firms, capital invested in manufacturing plants may represent less than 50 percent of the true economic capital of the firm (Table 4). First, advertising and other promotion activities are chosen partly according to their ability to augment revenues over long periods of time.[1] Various studies indicate that the economic life of advertising capital ranges from less than one year in one industry to more than ten years in some,[2]

---

[1] See Yale Brozen, ed., *Advertising and Society* (New York: New York University Press, 1974).

[2] See Yoram Peles, "Rates of Amortization of Advertising Expenditures," *Journal of Political Economy*, vol. 79, no. 5 (September/October 1971), pp. 1032-1058; Kristian Palda, "The Measurement of Cumulative Advertising Effects," *Journal of Business*, vol. 38, no. 5 (April 1965), pp. 162-179; Lester Telser, "Advertising and Cigarettes," *Journal of Political Economy*, vol. 70, no. 5 (October 1962), pp. 471-499; Roy W. Jastram, "A Treatment of Distributed Lags in the Theory of Advertising Expenditure," *Journal of Marketing*, vol. 20, no. 1 (July 1955), pp. 36-46; Neil H. Borden, *The Economic Effects of Advertising* (Homewood, Ill.: Richard D. Irwin, Inc., 1952), pp. 105, 135, 137, 140; Sidney Hollander, "A Rationale for Advertising Expenditures," *Harvard Business Review*, vol. 27, no. 1 (January 1949), pp. 79-87; M. L. Vidale and H. B. Wolfe, "An Operations Research Study of Sales Response to Advertising," *Operations Research*, vol. 5,

Table 4

ANNUAL PHYSICAL AND INTANGIBLE CAPITAL
EXPENDITURES IN THE PHARMACEUTICAL
PREPARATIONS INDUSTRY,[a] 1960–1972

(in millions of dollars)

Year	New Plant and New Equipment	R & D[b]	Advertising[c]
1960	85.1	196.1	108.7
1961	86.4	215.9	113.3
1962	71.5	224.8	126.9
1963	89.3	248.2	140.9
1964	102.7	254.3	157.1
1965	122.6	304.2	185.1
1966	133.8	344.2	196.8
1967	169.6	377.9	215.1
1968	185.3	410.4	223.4
1969	247.6	464.1	257.1
1970	250.1	518.6	280.5
1971	195.7	576.5	286.4
1972	166.7	600.7	272.0

[a] Standard Industrial Classification (SIC) 2834.

[b] Figures do not include research and development outlays for veterinary pharmaceutical research.

[c] Computed from data for all chemicals (SIC 28).

Source: U.S. Department of Commerce, *Annual Survey of Manufacturers* (Washington, D.C.: U.S. Government Printing Office, various dates); Pharmaceutical Manufacturers Association, *Annual Survey Reports* (Washington, D.C.: various dates); and Bureau of the Census, *Statistical Abstract of the United States* (Washington, D.C.: U.S. Government Printing Office, various dates).

depending on such factors as the media used, the scope and clarity of the information, the nature of the product, and the life of the product itself. In the pharmaceutical industry, where new products are patentable and do not become obsolete or reach a commodity status for ten to twenty years, advertising and other promotional

no. 3 (June 1957), pp. 370-381; D. S. Tull, *An Examination of the Hypothesis that Advertising Has a Lagged Effect on Sales* (Ph.D. diss., University of Chicago, 1956); and Marc Nerlove and Frederick Waugh, "Advertising without Supply Control: Some Implications of a Study of the Advertising of Oranges," *Journal of Farm Economics*, vol. 43, no. 5 (October 1961), pp. 813-837.

activities would be directed toward long-term effects. It is also likely that information received through direct personal interaction has a more durable effect and correspondingly longer economic life than information received through print or broadcast promotion. The pharmaceutical industry channels the majority of its promotion expenditures into direct personal interaction. The lower bound on the economic life of pharmaceutical advertising and promotion activities is, therefore, likely to be at least three years. The depreciation periods for advertising and promotion expenditures for a typical pharmaceutical manufacturing enterprise will thus be (conservatively) set at three years.

More important, pharmaceutical enterprises allocate large expenditures for research on and development of new products. These expenditures produce no revenues for some years—then, if successful, they provide revenues over the remainder of the product's life cycle. A small amount of each research dollar is allocated for basic research with no immediate commercial application. In most pharmaceutical firms, basic research budgets are allocated to investigations covering broad therapeutic areas, to the synthesis of naturally occurring pharmacologically active compounds, and to related investigations of compounds. The remainder of the funds allocated to general research activities are more specifically directed to development of products which, it is hoped, will become marketable. The preliminary testing, the evaluation, the additional testing to meet FDA regulations, and other related activities are included in this development stage. Once a compound becomes a commercial product, research activity on that compound does not cease automatically. Additional research activities continue during the remainder of the compound's economic life, including (but not limited to) the introduction of improved manufacturing procedures, new quality control, and the identification of new uses, new dosages, and the effects and interactions with other drugs. Estimates of the average life cycle of a pharmaceutical product, including research and development time, range from twenty to thirty years.[3] A representative life cycle for research expenditures, displayed in Figure 1, shows basic research accumulating for ten to twelve years and development for five to seven years before the compound is marketed. Since most compounds can be patented and the remaining patent life after a compound reaches the market is usually ten to

---

[3] See Harold Clymer, "The Changing Costs and Risks of Pharmaceutical Innovation," in Joseph Cooper, *Economics of Drug Innovation* (Washington, D.C.: American University, 1970), and Lewis Sarett, "Impact of FDA on Industrial Research and Development," in Richard Landau, *Regulating New Drugs* (Chicago: University of Chicago Press, 1973).

Figure 1

ECONOMIC LIFE CYCLE FOR RESEARCH AND DEVELOPMENT EXPENDITURES

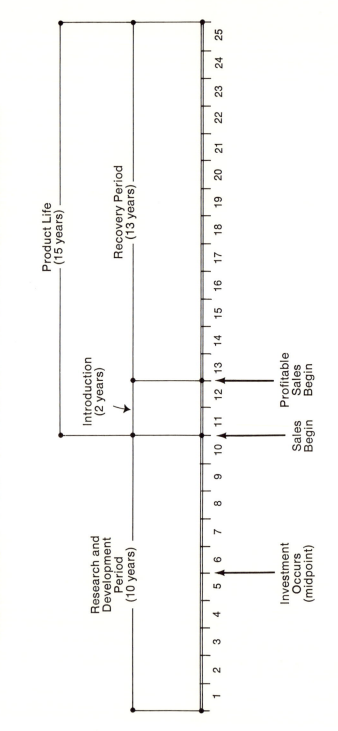

Source: Vernon A. Mund, "The Return on Investment of the Innovative Pharmaceutical Firm," in Joseph Cooper, ed., *The Economics of Drug Innovation* (Washington, D.C.: American University, 1970), p. 131.

44

twelve years,[4] the total life cycle is approximately twenty-five to thirty years. In our initial corrections for the pharmaceutical enterprise's research expenditures, we will choose a minimum twenty-six-year life for basic research and sixteen-year economic life for development. Basic research expenditures are assumed to accumulate for eleven years and development expenditures for the last six of the eleven years before the compound is marketed.[5] When data are not available for basic research, expenditures for basic research are assumed to be 16 percent of total research expenditures.[6]

Table 5 gives the current dollar receipts, current operating expenses (including depreciation on plant and equipment), capital outlays (including advertising, other promotion, and research and development), uncorrected pretax profit, taxes, and uncorrected profits for a pharmaceutical manufacturing enterprise for the years 1965 through 1974.[7] While most comparisons of current expenses to sales or other relationships for each year are valid, interyear comparisons will be biased by inflation and will therefore not reflect the real use and exchange of resources and goods. For example, the uncorrected profit in 1965 was $37,600,000 in 1965 dollars. Before this amount can be usefully compared with the 1973 uncorrected profit—$129,700,000 in 1973 dollars—either the 1973 or the 1965 amount must be adjusted for price level changes. Using 1973 as the base year for a price index, we adjust the 1965 uncorrected profit for inflation by dividing it by the price index for that year ($37,600,000 divided by .717, with the .717 from Appendix A). The 1965 uncorrected profit is then $52,441,000 in 1973 dollars.

In Table 6 uncorrected profits have been inflated by the appropriate index from Appendix A. Book manufacturing assets and net worth for this representative firm are also adjusted to 1973 dollars. The conventional accounting rate of return on net worth and on assets can thus easily be calculated by dividing the entries in column 2 (original profit) by those in column 3 (net worth) and column 4 (assets), to obtain the accounting rate of return on net worth (column 5) and assets (column 6) respectively. The average accounting

---

[4] D. Schwartzman, *Innovation in the Pharmaceutical Industry* (Baltimore: Johns Hopkins Press, 1976), chapter 9. If a product does not become obsolete before its patent expires, it may continue to contribute a modest return to research and development investment.

[5] Recent experience with the 1962 drug amendments indicates the period of accumulation should be longer.

[6] See Table 14 in Chapter 4.

[7] Capital expenditures, for reasons to be explained later, are shown for longer periods.

Table 5
FINANCIAL DATA FROM A FIRM WITH LARGE INTANGIBLE CAPITAL
(millions of current dollars)

Year	Sales	Current Expenses	Intangible Capital Outlays		Uncorrected Pretax Profit	Taxes	Uncorrected Profit
			Advertising and promotion	Research and development			
1949				3.5			
1950				4.1			
1951				5.0			
1952				6.4			
1953				7.0			
1954				8.7			
1955				9.6			
1956				11.2			
1957				13.2			
1958				15.7			
1959			32.5	18.3			
1960			33.7	19.7			
1961			36.1	20.2			
1962			39.2	22.3			
1963			45.3	25.5			
1964			48.7	27.9			
1965	316.6	151.0	57.0	31.6	77.0	39.4	37.6
1966	366.7	176.8	66.8	33.9	89.2	43.5	45.7
1967	408.4	199.5	76.5	40.7	91.7	42.5	49.2
1968	479.6	226.4	84.7	47.6	120.9	57.8	63.1
1969	537.2	252.6	94.5	54.8	135.3	61.6	73.7
1970	592.3	294.4	101.7	61.0	135.2	54.9	80.3
1971	723.3	378.6	141.6	67.5	135.6	51.9	83.7
1972	819.7	412.8	150.4	74.3	182.2	74.2	108.0
1973	972.5	471.6	179.4	83.3	238.2	108.5	129.7
1974	1,111.5	557.5	194.6	93.3	266.1	123.9	142.2

Source: Eli Lilly and Company, *Annual Reports*, various years, and unpublished historical company data for R & D (1949, 1950) and advertising and promotion (1959).

46

Table 6

PHARMACEUTICAL MANUFACTURERS' RATES OF RETURN ON NET WORTH AND ASSETS BASED ON BOOK VALUE[a]

(millions of constant dollars)

Year	Uncor-rected Profit	Net Worth	Assets	Uncorrected Rate of Return Net worth	Assets
1955		202.454	244.939		
1956		227.043	290.639		
1957		247.475	312.987		
1958		255.983	308.974		
1959		258.523	306.250		
1960		261.702	302.128		
1961		267.664	316.809		
1962		270.881	321.165		
1963		281.054	341.168		
1964		297.013	364.865		
1965	52.441	321.060	409.205	16.334%	12.815%
1966	61.673	336.572	434.548	18.324	14.193
1967	66.307	387.466	505.121	17.113	13.127
1968	82.917	451.905	604.599	18.348	13.714
1969	93.173	513.654	685.082	18.139	13.600
1970	97.927	571.098	829.146	17.147	11.811
1971	98.936	627.069	935.816	15.778	10.572
1972	122.172	699.434	981.787	17.467	12.444
1973	129.700	730.200	1,020.300	17.762	12.712
1974	119.596	713.625	1,064.003	16.759	11.240

[a] Computed using 1973 dollars.

Source: Net worth and assets from Eli Lilly and Company, *Annual Reports*, various years. Uncorrected profits computed from current dollar values in Table 5.

rate of return during this period was 17.32 percent (with a variance of .67 percent) when based on net worth, and 12.62 percent (with a variance of 1.17 percent) when based on assets. If yearly ratios are weighted by assets in each year, the average accounting rate of return becomes 12.38 percent. Uncorrected profits, net worth, and assets based on book valuations are all adjusted by the wholesale price index for each year without adjustment of depreciation expense (other than the adjustment implicit in the adjustment of profit figures). Consequently, there is no change from the accounting rate-of-return ratios based on current dollars. On the other hand, this price level adjustment permits direct comparisons of profits (assuming that a depreciation expense adjustment would be trifling),[8] net worth, or assets for any combination of years.

Effects of Capitalization

The effects of capitalizing and depreciating advertising, promotion, and research and development expenditures in the pharmaceutical firm are shown in Table 7. All amounts are expressed in constant 1973 dollars. The importance of price level correction becomes apparent when we recognize that some research expenditures may not begin depreciating (that is, may not begin being charged against the revenues they produce) for ten years or more after the outlay occurs, inasmuch as the research is not applied to revenue-producing activity for that length of time.

Economic rates of return on net worth and assets, corrected for capitalization of intangible assets and expressed in constant 1973 dollars, are shown in the two rightmost columns of Table 7. Current sales less current accounting expenses (operating costs, depreciation on physical plant and equipment, overhead, advertising, marketing, and research expenditures) are given in column 2 of Table 7. Column 3 shows current capital expenditures for advertising and promotion. The economic depreciation for these activities is shown in column 4 where straight-line depreciation is used, and advertising and promotion are depreciated for three years. The current capital value and balance for future depreciation of these activities is given in column 5. This current capital value is to be added to inflation-adjusted net worth and assets of the firm.

The current year's basic research and development (where basic research is stipulated to be 16 percent of the research budget) do not

---

[8] We have made no adjustment for depreciation expenses on physical plant, assuming that it would be trifling. Where it is large relative to reported profits, adjustment from original book dollars to current dollars could have an important effect. For example, suppose physical plant were acquired in one year at a cost of $20 million. Assuming no other physical plant currently in use a decade later, $10 million in current revenues, $7 million in current operating costs and taxes, and $1 million in depreciation based on book cost and a twenty-year life (straight-line depreciation), the $2 million in profit on the $10 million of depreciated cost would yield a 20 percent accounting rate of return (assuming no working capital were required). If replacement costs for plant were to have doubled, the depreciated value of the plant in current dollars would be $20 million, current depreciation would become $2 million annually, and current profits would be reduced to $1 million. For this reason, retrospective revaluation of past profits to current dollars will still leave an overstatement in the growth of profits if the depreciation adjustment is more than trifling.

Table 7
PHARMACEUTICAL MANUFACTURERS' CORRECTED RATES OF RETURN
(millions of 1973 dollars)

Year (1)	Sales Less Current Expenses (2)	Advertising and Promotion			General Research		Corrected Profits (8)	Corrected Net Worth (9)	Corrected Assets (10)	Corrected Rates of Return	
		Initial Outlays (3)	Depreciation[a] (4)	Balance (5)	Capital[b] (6)	Depreciation[c] (7)				Net worth (11)	Assets (12)
1955					8.918	.892		297.215	339.700		
1956					10.051	1.897		345.882	409.478		
1957					11.007	2.998		393.433	458.946		
1958			15.388	30.777	14.474	4.445		432.827	485.819		
1959		46.165	31.322	47.256	16.051	6.050		501.345	549.072		
1960		47.801	48.464	50.217	22.654	8.224		558.034	598.459		
1961		51.425	51.636	54.263	24.994	10.621		604.531	653.677		
1962		55.682	57.212	61.581	28.141	13.323		651.864	702.148		
1963		64.530	63.162	67.693	32.785	16.453		713.469	773.583		
1964		69.275	71.101	76.090	38.205	20.109		781.932	849.784		
1965	230.962	79.498	79.640	86.598	44.792	23.493	96.353	864.379	952.524	11.147%	10.116%
1966	256.275	90.148	90.915	98.783	48.304	27.094	108.365	941.165	1,039.141	11.514	10.428
1967	281.536	103.100	101.516	108.567	50.417	30.782	120.199	1,064.078	1,181.733	11.296	10.171
1968	332.720	111.301	111.290	116.746	55.833	34.628	141.783	1,206.236	1,358.930	11.754	10.433
1969	359.798	119.469	118.265	122.506	64.265	39.109	156.864	1,350.850	1,522.278	11.612	10.305
1970	363.293	124.024	136.956	152.925	70.925	43.815	165.409	1,493.943	1,751.992	11.072	9.441
1971	407.447	167.376	153.845	169.216	78.341	49.032	183.914	1,665.479	1,974.226	11.043	9.316
1972	460.294	170.136	172.304	176.312	81.215	54.239	205.335	1,844.058	2,126.411	11.135	9.656
1973	500.900	179.400	172.304	176.312	96.086	60.532	209.478	1,969.534	2,259.634	10.636	9.270
1974	465.938	163.667	171.068	168.911	109.662	67.617	189.533	2,024.621	2,374.999	9.361	7.980

[a] Advertising and promotion are depreciated for three years.
[b] Basic research accumulates for eleven years and development accumulates for six years.
[c] Basic research is depreciated for fifteen years and development is depreciated for ten years.
Source: Computed from statistics given in Tables 5 and 6.

yield revenues for the current year. They are, therefore, not depreciated in the current year. On the other hand, these activities do represent an asset—conceivably, information collected could be sold—and are, therefore, added to corrected net worth and assets. Moreover, until the asset begins to yield revenues to the firm, the research expenditures accumulate in value at the opportunity cost of capital (specified as 10 percent unless otherwise stated). This period of accumulation is six years for development and eleven years for basic research. When the period of accumulation of research capital is completed, the research capital is transferred to the general research capital account (column 6 in Table 7). Thus, the original $3.5 million in research and development is price-adjusted to $5.993 million in 1973 dollars and accumulated for its economic life.[9] Since development expenditures accumulate for six years, 84 percent of the accumulated 1949 research and development outlays or $8.92 million may be reckoned as capital in 1955. Depreciation of general research for each year is shown in column 7 and the balance of the undepreciated research and development is added to adjusted net worth and assets. In 1955 depreciation of development is $0.89 million, yielding a balance of $8.03 million in research capital.

The corrected profits for each year are found by adding the original profits and the difference between current advertising, marketing, direct research, and general research, on the one hand, and the depreciation of these accounts in the current year adjusted for changes in taxes (assumed to be 50 percent) plus the implicit unrealized income on capital accumulation on the other hand.[10] The corrected rates of return on net worth and assets are given in columns 11 and 12 respectively.

Comparisons between the accounting and corrected rates of return show striking differences. For example, the accounting rate of return on net worth in constant dollars (1973 = 100) for 1966, 1969, and 1970 exceeds 18 percent.[11] The economic rates of return, for the same years, however, are less than 12 percent.[12] The average rate of return for the last ten years shows a similar bias. From 1965 to 1974, the average accounting rate of return was 17.3 percent on net worth and 12.6 percent on assets (12.4 percent when weighted by assets).[13] During the same period the estimated economic rate of return averaged

---

9 See Appendix A for the wholesale price index.
10 See [2] in Chapter 2.
11 See Table 6.
12 See Table 7.
13 Calculated from Table 6.

11.1 percent on net worth and 9.7 percent on assets (9.5 percent when weighted by corrected assets).[14]

Some indirect evidence of the validity of capitalizing and depreciating advertising, marketing, and direct research is provided when we examine the variance in the rate of return with and without capital outlay adjustments. When markets are relatively competitive, entry and exit—or expansion and contraction by existing firms—will cause the rate of return to move towards the opportunity cost of capital, adjusted for risk.[15] Risk, information and transaction costs, and disequilibrium forces, however, ensure that some variance in rates of return will occur. In addition, if rates of return contain systematic biases for some industries, measured variance will tend to be larger than the variance based on corrected rates of return. Since the corrections given above are designed to match economic costs with returns, we would expect calculated variances to decline after the appropriate corrections have been made. An examination of the variance in estimated rates of return when advertising, marketing, and direct research are capitalized confirms the accuracy of this expectation. The variance of the rate of return on net worth for 1965 to 1974 falls from 0.67 to 0.41 percent when capitalization is made. Similarly, the variance of the rate of return on assets falls from 1.17 to 0.52 percent (and from 1.17 to 0.58 percent when weighted by corrected assets) for the same period.

Modification of Assumptions: A Sensitivity Analysis

These results hold even with modifications of the price level adjustments, economic life cycles for research expenditures, depreciation periods, and the opportunity cost of capital. First, if calculations are based on current dollar amounts rather than price-level-adjusted amounts, there is little change in the outcome. With identical capitalization and depreciation assumptions, the average economic rate of return on net worth using current dollars is 11.9 percent for 1965 to 1974, or only 0.8 percentage points higher than the average using price-adjusted data.[16]

---

[14] Calculated from Table 7.

[15] See Lester Telser, "The Supply Response to Shifting Demand in the Ethical Pharmaceutical Industry," and Douglas Cocks, "Product Innovation and the Dynamic Elements of Competition in the Ethical Pharmaceutical Industry," in Helms, *Drug Development and Marketing*.

[16] The 1965-1974 average economic rate of return on unweighted assets rises 0.7 percentage points to 10.4 percent and 0.8 percentage points to 10.3 percent when weighted by adjusted assets using current expenditures.

Table 8

EFFECTS OF ALTERNATIVE CAPITAL OUTLAY CORRECTIONS
ON AVERAGE RATES OF RETURN, 1965–1974
(in percentages)

Number of Years Depreciated	Net worth	Corrected Rate of Return Unweighted assets	Weighted assets
Advertising and promotion [a]			
1 year	17.32	12.62	12.38
2 years	15.87	11.92	11.68
3 years	14.81	11.39	11.15
4 years	14.00	10.98	10.75
5 years	13.39	10.65	10.44
10 years	11.70	9.76	9.52
Research, Development [b]			
2 years, 2 years	16.47	12.21	11.97
5 years, 5 years	14.73	11.33	11.10
10 years, 5 years	14.43	11.18	10.96
10 years, 10 years	13.14	10.48	10.29
15 years, 10 years	12.99	10.40	10.21
15 years, 15 years	12.29	10.01	9.84

[a] No research or development depreciation.
[b] No advertising or promotion depreciation.
Source: Computed from statistics given in Tables 5 and 6 using 1973 dollars.

Second, the effects of modifying the depreciation period for advertising and promotion are shown in Table 8. As predicted, longer economic lives are generally accompanied by lower average economic rates of return.[17] When advertising and promotion are depreciated for three years, the ten-year average return on net worth (with price corrections) is 14.8 percent. This falls to 13.4 percent and 11.7 percent when the depreciation period is lengthened to five and ten years, respectively. Average rates of return on both unweighted and weighted assets follow a similar pattern with longer advertising and promotion depreciation periods. Table 8 also shows the consequences of modifying the research and development depreciation period when no

---

[17] If the growth rate of advertising and promotion is very high, the average rate of return could increase with longer economic lives.

Table 9
EFFECTS OF ALTERNATIVE CAPITAL EXPENSE CORRECTIONS FOR BASIC RESEARCH AND DEVELOPMENT ON AVERAGE RATES OF RETURN, 1965–1974
(in percentages)

Capital Expense Corrections (years accumulated or depreciated)	Corrected Rate of Return		
	Net worth	Unweighted assets	Weighted assets
Basic research accumulation (6) Development accumulation (6) Basic research depreciation (10) Development depreciation (5)	12.33	10.50	10.35
Basic research accumulation (6) Development accumulation (6) Basic research depreciation (10) Development depreciation (10)	11.77	10.14	9.99
Basic research accumulation (6) Development accumulation (6) Basic research depreciation (15) Development depreciation (10)	11.71	10.11	9.96
Basic research accumulation (6) Development accumulation (6) Basic research depreciation (15) Development depreciation (15)	11.44	9.95	9.78
Basic research accumulation (11) Development accumulation (6) Basic research depreciation (10) Development depreciation (5)	12.25	10.51	10.35
Basic research accumulation (11) Development accumulation (6) Basic research depreciation (10) Development depreciation (10)	11.72	10.17	10.01
Basic research accumulation (11) Development accumulation (6) Basic research depreciation (15) Development depreciation (10)	11.71	10.17	10.00
Basic research accumulation (11) Development accumulation (6) Basic research depreciation (15) Development depreciation (15)	11.45	10.01	9.83
Basic research accumulation (11) Development accumulation (11) Basic research depreciation (10) Development depreciation (5)	11.78	10.41	10.24
Basic research accumulation (11) Development accumulation (11) Basic research depreciation (10) Development depreciation (10)	11.55	10.28	10.08

Table 9 (continued)

Capital Expense Corrections (years accumulated or depreciated)	Corrected Rate of Return		
	Net worth	Unweighted assets	Weighted assets
Basic research accumulation (11) Development accumulation (11) Basic research depreciation (15) Development depreciation (10)	11.54	10.28	10.07
Basic research accumulation (11) Development accumulation (11) Basic research depreciation (15) Development depreciation (15)	11.50	10.27	10.04

Source: Computed from statistics given in Tables 5 and 6 using 1973 dollars.

capital accumulation is present. Increasing the economic life of research and development expenditures generally lowers the average economic rate of return. Equally important, with each of these various assumptions, the variance of returns is lower than the variances calculated with no depreciation of advertising and promotion or rerearch and development expenses.

Third, lengthening the total economic life cycle by increasing the period for accumulation and depreciation also lowers yearly and ten-year-average economic rates of return from the levels of the accounting rates of return. For example, Table 9 shows that the 1965–1974 average economic rate of return on net worth comes out to 11.7 percent when a sixteen-year life cycle for research and development is chosen and 11.5 percent when a twenty-six-year life cycle is chosen. Moreover, Table 9 reveals little variation in the ten-year-average economic rates of return for relatively large changes in the economic life cycle, though all variations yield rates of return below the uncorrected accounting rates of return. Furthermore, the variance of economic rates of return on net worth (and on unweighted and weighted assets) is always lower than the variance for the uncorrected rate of return.

Fourth, as Table 10 shows, combining capitalization of advertising and promotion with capitalization of basic research and development produces both a general lowering of yearly and average rates of return and a reduction in the variance of the rate of return. For example, increasing the total economic life cycle by five years (development depreciation lengthened to ten years) when advertising and promotion are depreciated for three years lowers the estimated ten-year average rate of return on net worth from 11.5 percent to 11.1

Table 10

COMBINED EFFECTS OF ALTERNATIVE CAPITAL EXPENSE
CORRECTIONS ON AVERAGE RATES OF RETURN, 1965–1974
(in percentages)

Capital Expense Corrections (years accumulated or depreciated)	Corrected Rate of Return		
	Net worth	Unweighted assets	Weighted assets
Basic research accumulation (11) Development accumulation (6) Advertising/promotion depreciation (3) Basic research depreciation (10) Development depreciation (5)	11.49	10.00	9.83
Basic research accumulation (11) Development accumulation (6) Advertising/promotion depreciation (3) Basic research depreciation (10) Development depreciation (10)	11.07	9.71	9.54
Basic research accumulation (11) Development accumulation (6) Advertising/promotion depreciation (3) Basic research depreciation (15) Development depreciation (10)	11.06	9.71	9.54
Basic research accumulation (11) Development accumulation (6) Advertising/promotion depreciation (3) Basic research depreciation (15) Development depreciation (15)	10.85	9.58	9.39
Basic research accumulation (11) Development accumulation (6) Advertising/promotion depreciation (4) Basic research depreciation (10) Development depreciation (5)	11.22	9.81	9.64
Basic research accumulation (11) Development accumulation (6) Advertising/promotion depreciation (4) Basic research depreciation (10) Development depreciation (10)	10.82	9.55	9.37
Basic research accumulation (11) Development accumulation (6) Advertising/promotion depreciation (4) Basic research depreciation (15) Development depreciation (15)	10.62	9.43	9.24
Basic research accumulation (11) Development accumulation (6) Advertising/promotion depreciation (5) Basic research depreciation (10) Development depreciation (10)	10.62	9.41	9.24
Basic research accumulation (11) Development accumulation (6) Advertising/promotion depreciation (5) Basic research depreciation (15) Development depreciation (15)	10.45	9.30	9.12

Source: Calculated from statistics given in Tables 5 and 6 using 1973 dollars.

Table 11

EFFECTS OF ALTERNATIVE OPPORTUNITY COSTS OF CAPITAL ON AVERAGE RATES OF RETURN, 1965–1974

(in percentages)

Opportunity Cost of Capital (interest rate)	Corrected Rate of Return		
	Net worth [a]	Unweighted assets [a]	Weighted assets [a]
10.0	11.06	9.71	9.54
11.0	11.13	9.80	9.62
12.0	11.20	9.89	9.72
13.0	11.27	9.99	9.81
14.0	11.34	10.08	9.90
15.0	11.41	10.17	10.00
15.0, 10.0 [b]	11.18	9.87	9.69

[a] Based on 1973 constant dollars with replacement valuations of capital. Basic research accumulates for eleven years and development for six years. Advertising and promotion are depreciated for three years, basic research for fifteen years, and development for ten years.

[b] Represents 15 percent for basic research and 10 percent for development.

Source: Computed from statistics given in Tables 5 and 6.

percent. Again the variance of economic rates of return is lower than the variance of the accounting rate of return.

Fifth, the effects from re-specifying the opportunity cost of capital are trifling. Changes in the opportunity cost of capital do not have any significant impact on the average economic rates of return. When the opportunity cost of capital is raised from 10 to 15 percent, the inflation-adjusted ten-year average economic rate of return increases from 11.1 percent to 11.4 percent (see Table 11).

Finally, other corrections—such as replacing the accounting depreciation schedules with schedules that more closely represent true economic depreciation—might increase accuracy but are unlikely to alter the major general effects described above. It should be noted that combinations of the changes suggested above are generally additive in that the individual effects maintain their expected directions. Table 10 shows, for example, that increasing both the length of advertising and of direct and general research life cycles lowers rates of return more than either single correction.

It should also be noted that under certain conditions corrected rates of return will be higher than uncorrected rates. For example, comparisons between corrected and uncorrected rates of return for the years when capitalization begins may not be valid unless there were no prior advertising and promotion or research and development capital expenditures—this because the corrected profits in expression [2] will not include depreciation of previous capital expenditures. In addition, if these capital expenditures are rising rapidly, similar biases may be introduced. If the period under analysis is significantly longer than the economic life cycles, and if the earliest years are omitted from comparisons of corrected and uncorrected rates of return, these biases can be decreased.

4
RATES OF RETURN: VARIATIONS AND POLICY DECISIONS

The application of correction techniques to a particular firm or industry is necessary for obtaining better measurements of the firm's or industry's real activities. The corrections that are applied to one industry must also be applied to others in order to make valid inter-industry comparisons of rates of return and the relative attractiveness of investment in each industry. Before these corrections are applied, the expected (or hypothesized) outcomes must be identified.

Variations in Manufacturing Rates of Return

Differences among rates of return in various industries are the product of many factors. First, the observed rates at any time are dispersed because industries are rarely in static equilibrium for long periods. Second, there may be differences in the nonmoney characteristics which would cause pecuniary rates to differ under competitive market conditions. Third, there are differences in "riskiness" among different industries, with higher average rates of return required for competitive viability in "riskier" industries. Fourth, differences in the quality of resources may cause variation in observed rates of return if superior resources are distributed unequally and earn unequal rents not completely capitalized on the books of the firms owning and using them. Fifth, entry barriers such as those erected by government regulation could cause observed rates of return in some industries to be higher than in others. Finally, differences in rates of return can exist whenever there are systematic errors in measurement differentially affecting firms in some industries.

Given these factors, it would be highly unlikely that observed rates of return among firms within an industry or for all industries

Table 12

ADVERTISING AS PERCENTAGE OF NET SALES,
1949–1971, BY INDUSTRY

Industry	Advertising as Percentage of Net Sales
Pharmaceuticals	3.7
Chemicals	3.7
Foods	2.3
Electrical machinery	1.6
Rubber products	1.5
Office machinery	1.0
Motor vehicles	0.8
Paper	0.7
Petroleum	0.5
Ferrous metals	0.3
Aerospace	0.3

Source: U.S. Bureau of the Census, *Statistical Abstract of the United States* (Washington, D.C.: U.S. Government Printing Office, various dates), and U.S. Treasury, *Statistics of Income: Corporate Income Tax Returns,* various issues.

would be equal. If any one or more of these factors can be eliminated or reduced, observed rates of return should tend to move closer together if markets are competitive. This study has concentrated on reducing the biases from current measurement techniques. If these biases have been reduced and markets are competitive, one would expect a narrowing of calculated rates of return.

A sample of sixty-nine firms representing eleven industries was chosen to test this hypothesis. These firms and industries are shown in Appendix B. To incorporate proper economic life cycles and to reduce the problems associated with disequilibrium forces, data for each firm from 1949 through 1973 were collected from Moody's *Industrial Manual.* Average industry advertising expenditures were taken from the *Statistical Abstract* and U.S. Treasury *Statistics of Income,* and average company research and development expenditures for each were obtained from the National Science Foundation (NSF). Tables 12 and 13 give these amounts as a percentage of net sales. Whenever research and development expenditures were not available

Table 13
RESEARCH AND DEVELOPMENT EXPENDITURES
AND SALES, 1961–1971, BY INDUSTRY[a]
(dollars in millions)

Industry	R & D Expenditures	Sales of R & D Firms	R & D as a Percentage of Sales
Pharmaceuticals	4,167	78,834	5.3
Electrical machinery	21,376	590,420	3.6
Aerospace	12,025	343,145	3.5
Chemicals	13,560	438,982	3.1
Office machinery	14,210	463,455	3.1
Motor vehicles	14,704	581,814	2.5
Rubber products	2,201	132,676	1.7
Paper products	1,702	188,949	0.9
Petroleum	5,431	625,902	0.9
Ferrous metals	1,819	268,227	0.7
Foods[b]	2,293	584,495	0.4

[a] Computed using 1973 constant dollars.
[b] Data not available for 1963.
Source: Calculated from statistics reported in National Science Foundation, *Research and Development in Industry, 1971,* NSF 73-305 (Washington, D.C.: NSF, 1971).

for a firm in Moody's, the industry average in Table 13 was used. A similar rule was used for advertising expenditures.

To determine the amount of basic research and development, industry data from NSF surveys for several years were price-adjusted and averaged. The results are shown in Table 14. The period of accumulation for development expenditures in each industry was estimated from several industry sources (see Table 15) with an additional five years added for basic research expenditures.

Average accounting rates of return for 1959–1973 were computed for each company. An industry average for each of eleven industries is shown in Table 16. An economic life of three years for advertising was chosen to correct for advertising and promotion biases and a ten-year period of depreciation was specified for basic research, with a five-year period for development. The pharmaceutical industry was assigned a fifteen-year depreciation period for basic research and

Table 14
BASIC AND TOTAL RESEARCH EXPENDITURES, 1960–1971, BY INDUSTRY

Industry	Expenditures (in millions of 1973 dollars)		Basic Research as a Percentage of R & D Expenditures
	Basic research	Total R & D	
Pharmaceuticals	784	4,890	16.0
Chemicals	2,007	17,388	11.5
Petroleum	535	6,241	8.6
Foods a	209	2,485	8.4
Ferrous metals b	67	918	7.3
Rubber products c	85	2,074	4.1
Electrical machinery	2,019	55,367	3.6
Paper products d	43	1,710	2.5
Motor vehicles b	219	8,955	2.4
Office machinery	395	19,642	2.0
Aerospace	1,018	79,686	1.3

a Data not available for 1962.
b Data not available for 1966-1971.
c Data not available for 1964, 1965, and 1971.
d Data not available for 1960.
Source: Calculated from statistics reported in *Research and Development in Industry, 1971* (see Table 13) using 1973 constant dollars.

a ten-year period for development. This modification was chosen to correct for conditions specific to the pharmaceutical industry.[1] As predicted, the corrected average rate of return significantly decreases for those industries which were relatively capital-intensive in advertising-promotion and research-development expenditures. The pharmaceutical and electrical industries, which spend relatively more on advertising and promotion (see Table 12) and on research and

---

[1] The creation and development of products takes a longer period of time than in other industries, hence entry (*de novo* or by expansion) involves a longer period of time. When combined with the patentability of ethical drugs, the effective life of products in this industry becomes significantly longer than the average in other industries. See Sam Peltzman, *Regulation of Pharmaceutical Innovation* (Washington, D.C.: American Enterprise Institute, 1974), and Schwartzman, *Expected Return from Pharmaceutical Research.*

Table 15

EXPECTED AVERAGE RESEARCH AND DEVELOPMENT PAYOUT PERIODS, BY INDUSTRY

Industry	Average Years
Pharmaceutical	6
Petroleum	5
Aerospace	4
Chemicals	4
Rubber products	4
Paper products	4
Ferrous metals	4
Electrical machinery	3
Office machinery	3
Motor vehicles	3
Foods	3

Source: Pharmaceutical average payout period was estimated from various sources reported in David Schwartzman, "Pharmaceutical R & D Expenditures and Rates of Return," in Robert Helms, ed., *Drug Development and Marketing* (Washington, D.C.: American Enterprise Institute for Public Policy Research, 1975), pp. 63-80. Average payout periods for all other industries were computed from data reported in Edward Mansfield, et al., *Research and Innovation in the Modern Corporation* (New York: W. W. Norton and Co., 1971), p. 7.

development (see Table 13), experience the largest change in their 1959–1973 average rates of return.

Overall, the estimated average rate of return in all industries falls from 11.2 to 9.6 percent. More important, the variance, when corrections have been made, falls substantially. Unfortunately, until one obtains better information about the economic life of advertising and the life cycle of research activities, the exact levels in each industry cannot be determined. This approach, however, casts serious doubt on previous studies in which interindustry differentials in rates of return were attributed to risk, entry barriers, concentration, and other related variables. Indeed, the results here suggest that if entry barriers exist, they are not particularly effective and that risk may have been overstated in previous inquiries.[2]

---

[2] The inclusion of these variables is beyond the scope of this study. For example, testing for the consequences of risk requires inclusion of either all or a significantly large random sample of the firms in the industry. For the pharmaceutical industry this entails knowledge about a large number of firms. Furthermore, data limitations further biased this sample towards the more successful larger firms.

Table 16

AVERAGE ACCOUNTING AND CORRECTED RATES OF RETURN ON NET WORTH, 1959–1973, BY INDUSTRY [a]

(in percentages)

Industry	Accounting Rates of Return	Corrected Rates of Return [b]
Pharmaceuticals	18.29	12.89 [c]
Electrical machinery	13.33	10.10
Foods	11.81	10.64
Petroleum	11.23	10.77
Chemicals	10.59	9.14
Motor vehicles	10.46	9.22
Paper	10.49	10.12
Rubber products	10.11	8.69
Office machinery	10.48	9.90
Aerospace	9.23	7.38
Ferrous metals	7.55	7.28
Average	11.2	9.6
Variance	7.5	2.5

[a] Calculated using 1973 constant dollars.

[b] Advertising and promotion depreciates for three years; basic research accumulates five years longer than development (given in Table 15); basic research depreciates for ten years and development for five years.

[c] Depreciation period for the pharmaceutical industry is fifteen years for basic research and ten years for development. This different cycle, however, changes the average by less than 0.5 percent.

Source: Calculated from individual firm data in Appendix B.

Finally, the methodology employed to correct accounting rates of return yields extremely robust results. This is true for variations in assumptions in this study and those assumptions employed by other studies of intangible capital (discussed in Appendix C). These independent studies further confirm the proposition that accounting rates of return are differentially biased.

Rates of Return and Public Policy Decisions

Policy makers should be interested in the results of this study. If the preliminary findings are representative of the changes to be expected from better information, then policy makers must be more careful than they have been in tracing the implications of changes in the basic constraints for any industry. A minor modification of the net rewards from innovation or other activities in any industry may have serious long-term consequences. Suppose, for example, that the government decides to impose a 100 percent tax on any accounting profits in excess of those equal to 10 percent of net worth. In Table 3, taxes for the fifth year would rise by $7 million to $24 million, leaving $10 million in aftertax profits or 10 percent of the $100 million in net worth. True economic profits in the fifth year, however, would fall to $13.97 million ($20.97 less $7.00 million), a return on net worth of 8.9 percent. Permanently increasing taxes would be equivalent to lowering A_t in equation [1]. This would reduce the value of previous investments and the expected values of future investments. In such a case, decision makers would have sharply reduced the number and amount of investments.

Modifications of the rules and regulations governing decision makers, such as the rule in expression [1], are capable of significantly altering individual decisions. For example, recent studies of the social security program indicate that it now constitutes the most important form of nonhousehold assets. Because social security reduces other forms of personal savings and because these forms would have been (and social security is not) available for industrial borrowing, future U.S. capital accumulation and income will have been reduced by as much as 15 percent.[3] A similar outcome is associated with the 1962 drug amendments which increased the length of time from initial research to NDA filing and also increased the length of time from filing to approval for marketing. They effectively lowered the present value of new pharmaceutical products by increasing the input period in the total economic life cycle by four to eight years. The simple mathematics of the reduced present value of the longer research life cycle are well demonstrated in recent studies.[4] The number of NDA filings has decreased and the number of research projects has declined. These results suggest that research and development activities are highly sensitive to new constraints.

[3] See Martin Feldstein, "Social Security, Induced Retirement, and Aggregate Capital Accumulation," *Journal of Political Economy*, vol. 82, no. 5 (September/October 1974), pp. 905-926.

[4] See Louis Lasagna and William Wardell, "The Rate of New Drug Discoveries," in Helms, *Drug Development and Marketing*; Sam Peltzman, "An Evaluation of Consumer Protection Legislation: The 1962 Drug Amendments," *Journal of Political Economy*, vol. 81, no. 5 (September/October 1973), pp. 1054-1056; and Schwartzman, *Expected Return from Pharmaceutical Research*.

This is especially important when one recognizes that the real cost of pharmaceutical research and development has increased more than 50 percent in the last decade.

When pharmaceutical or other firms are faced with reduced present values or lower economic rates of return, it is likely that the number of research and development projects will be curtailed. Unfortunately, this implies that both potential projects will be terminated and fewer new projects will be initiated. It is unlikely that government projects could be instituted to offset this. A recent study shows that the pharmaceutical industry is the primary force behind new chemical entities despite the large sums spent by the government and nonprofit organizations on health research.[5]

Public provision of goods and services does not appear to be a viable alternative. Evidence from the British experience with nationalization clearly demonstrates the problems inherent in public production. Without exception, standardized value-added in private industries has been more than three times as high per unit of input as the value-added in nationalized industries. In 1971, for example, in Britain the value of output per £100 of labor and capital was £99 for private manufacturing concerns and £67 for nationalized industries.[6] Marginal returns are also significantly higher for private manufacturing firms. Between 1948 and 1968 the increase in output from £100 fixed investment (with the appropriate adjustment for employment) for private manufacturing was more than three times the increase found in nationalized industries.[7] Experience over the longer run shows similar outcomes. The average rate of return for private industries over the eighteen-year period studied by the Polanyis is three and one-half times as large as the average for nationalized industries.

Equally important, policy makers should be aware of the external consequences of reduced pharmaceutical research.[8] Because pharmaceutical products have been an increasingly important source of foreign exchange, any long-run analysis of public policy outcomes should incorporate this general equilibrium result. Available evidence shows that research-and-development-intensive industries in the United

---

[5] Schwartzman, *Expected Return from Pharmaceutical Research.*

[6] George and Priscilla Polanyi, *Failing the Nation: The Record of the Nationalized Industries* (London: Fraser Ansbacher Ltd., 1974), p. 28.

[7] Ibid., p. 30.

[8] Henry Grabowski, *Drug Regulation and Innovation* (Washington, D.C.: American Enterprise Institute for Public Policy Research, 1976), chapter 3.

States have systematically increased their world market position.[9] Studies also show that the pharmaceutical industry is simultaneously the most research-intensive and produces the highest value-added per employee for all U.S. industries.[10] This high value-added reflects the large amount of implicit human capital in research and development.

Finally, some of the results from private research and development yield substantial benefits to other industries and to society. For example, the indirect knowledge concerning the interactions and processes of individual biological functions is greatly enhanced by pharmaceutical research.

[9] Donald Keesing, "The Impact of Research and Development on United States Trade," in Peter Kenen and Roger Lawrence, eds., *The Open Economy* (New York: Columbia University Press, 1968), p. 178.
[10] Donald Keesing, "Towards a Theoretically Satisfactory Indicator of Comparative Advantage," Research Center in Economic Growth, Stanford University, 1972.

APPENDIX A

Wholesale Price Index, 1949–1974

Year	Price Index (1973 = 100.0)	Year	Price Index (1973 = 100.0)
1949	58.4	1962	70.4
1950	60.7	1963	70.2
1951	67.6	1964	70.3
1952	65.8	1965	71.7
1953	64.9	1966	74.1
1954	65.0	1967	74.2
1955	65.2	1968	76.1
1956	67.3	1969	79.1
1957	69.3	1970	82.0
1958	70.2	1971	84.6
1959	70.4	1972	88.4
1960	70.5	1973	100.0
1961	70.2	1974	118.9

Source: Calculated from indexes reported in Council of Economic Advisers, *Economic Report of the President*, February 1975.

APPENDIX B

Industries and Firms Included
In Capital Expenditure Sample

Food and Kindred Products: Beatrice Foods Company; Borden, Incorporated; CPC International Inc.; General Foods Corporation; Kraftco; Standard Brands Incorporated, and Swift and Company.

Paper and Allied Products: Crown Zellerbach Corporation; Diamond International Corporation; Georgia-Pacific Corporation; St. Regis Paper Company, and Weyerhaeuser Company.

Industrial and Other Chemicals: Allied Chemical Corporation; Celanese Corporation; Dow Chemical Company; E. I. du Pont de Nemours & Company, Inc.; Inmont Corporation; Koppers Company, Inc.; Monsanto Company, and Union Carbide Corporation.

Pharmaceuticals and Medicines: Abbott Laboratories; Merck & Co., Inc.; Pfizer, Inc.; Rexall Drug and Chemical Company; Schering Corporation; SmithKline Corporation; Sterling Drug, Inc., and Warner-Lambert Company.

Petroleum: Continental Oil Company; Exxon Corporation; Gulf Oil Corporation; Mobil Oil Corporation; Phillips Petroleum Company; Shell Oil Company; Standard Oil Company of California, and Texaco, Inc.

Rubber Products: Firestone Tire and Rubber Company; General Tire and Rubber Company; B. F. Goodrich Company; Goodyear Tire and Rubber Company, and Uniroyal, Inc.

Ferrous Metals: Armco Steel Corporation; Bethlehem Steel Corporation; Inland Steel Company; Jones & Laughlin Steel Corporation; National Steel Corporation; Republic Steel Corporation, and United States Steel Corporation.

Office Machines and Computers: Addressograph Multigraph Corporation; Burroughs Corporation; International Business Machines Corporation; SCM Corporation, and Sperry Rand Corporation.

Electrical Machinery and Appliances: General Electric Company; Motorola Inc.; RCA Corporation; Westinghouse Electric Corporation, and Whirlpool Corporation.

Motor Vehicles: American Motors Corporation; Chrysler Corporation; Ford Motor Company; General Motors Corporation, and White Motor Corporation.

Aerospace: Boeing Commercial Airplane Company; Curtiss-Wright Corporation; Lockheed Aircraft Corporation; McDonnell Douglas Astronautics Company; Northrop Corporation, and United Technologies Corporation.

APPENDIX C

Previous Economic Rate-of-Return Studies

Biases in the accounting rate of return have previously been estimated in three separate studies by Harry Bloch, in the *Journal of Political Economy*, by Robert Ayanian, in the *Journal of Law and Economics*, and in *Drug Development and Marketing*. Both the Bloch and Ayanian (*Journal of Law and Economics*) studies limit intangible capital to advertising and investigate its effect on rates of return. The Bloch study uses a uniform depreciation period for advertising in all firms. The Ayanian study determines different depreciation periods in each industry for computing intangible capital and rates of return. Both studies find that the adjusted rates of return for the firms examined are lower than book rates of return (with one exception) and that there is a differential impact among companies. Table C-1, computed by Bloch, shows the original profit rates and estimated true rates for the ratio of net income after taxes plus interest on long-term debt to reported net worth plus long-term debt (P_1) and the ratio of net income after taxes to reported net worth (P_2). The respective estimates of the true rates of return are shown as $P_1{}^*$ and $P_2{}^*$. Table C-1 also shows the advertising-to-sales ratio for each firm (column 5) and average advertising assets in millions of dollars (column 6).

Table C-2 reproduces the results of the Ayanian study published in the *Journal of Law and Economics*. In column 1 an estimate of each firm's annual advertising retention ratio is given. Advertising as a percent of sales is shown in column 2 and the original accounting rate of return is given in column 3 for each firm. An estimation of the true (or corrected) rate of return for each firm is given in column 4.

The other Ayanian study (in *Drug Development and Marketing*) corrects for two types of intangible capital for drug companies, but

Table C-1
BOOK AND CORRECTED PROFIT RATES AND ADVERTISING-TO-SALES RATIOS FOR FOOD MANUFACTURING FIRMS, 1950–1953
(in percentages)

Company	Average Profit Rates				Advertising-to-Sales Ratio
	P_1	P_2	$P_1{}^*$	$P_2{}^*$	
Swift & Co.	6.5	7.2	5.8	6.3	0.37
Armour & Co.	5.1	5.8	4.9	5.4	0.27
Schenley Industries	6.4	8.6	5.7	7.0	2.50
National Dairy Products	9.9	13.0	8.8	10.9	0.92
Jos. Seagram & Sons	11.3	14.2	9.1	10.5	2.06
General Foods	10.7	12.5	7.2	7.7	4.03
National Distillers Products	6.4	8.0	5.8	6.9	1.96
Borden Co.	9.0	10.9	8.1	9.4	0.60
Coca-Cola Co.	16.6	16.8	12.5	12.6	2.23
National Biscuit Co.	12.3	12.5	10.7	10.8	1.28
Hiram Walker & Sons	13.7	14.0	11.3	11.4	1.14
Corn Products Refining	12.4	12.4	11.0	11.0	1.32
California Packing	8.1	9.2	7.5	8.2	1.13
Wilson & Co.	4.3	4.4	4.1	4.2	0.11
General Mills	9.4	9.7	6.0	6.1	3.24
Publicker Industries	4.1	4.1	4.1	4.1	1.57
H. J. Heinz	6.5	6.7	4.9	4.8	1.45
Standard Brands	8.3	8.4	5.3	5.3	1.94
Libby, McNeil, & Libby	6.5	7.8	5.2	5.8	1.11
Wesson Oil & Snowdrift	7.0	7.0	6.5	6.5	1.02
Pillsbury Mills	6.1	7.1	5.4	5.9	2.49
Pabst Brewing	11.1	12.1	9.6	10.3	1.75
Quaker Oats Co.	11.3	13.0	7.9	8.4	3.23
Ralston Purina Co.	10.6	12.3	8.4	9.3	0.63
Carnation Co.	10.5	12.4	9.0	10.1	1.01
Wm. Wrigley, Jr. Co.	15.8	15.8	11.4	11.4	5.73
Continental Baking Co.	9.8	12.3	7.6	8.9	1.16
Stokely-Van Camp	8.1	8.1	7.1	7.0	1.26
Sunshine Biscuits	15.2	15.2	13.0	13.0	1.07
Brown-Forman Distillers	9.3	12.4	8.0	9.6	3.68
Kellogg Co.	23.5	23.5	10.7	10.7	5.04
Pet Milk Co.	7.8	7.8	6.4	6.4	1.38
Best Foods	13.8	13.8	9.4	9.4	2.85
Geo. Hormel & Co.	8.7	10.0	7.3	8.0	0.46
Canada Dry Ginger Ale	8.5	9.6	6.1	6.4	3.70
Glenmore Distillers Co.	7.9	9.7	6.4	7.1	3.89
Hunt Foods	9.5	9.9	8.8	9.0	3.64
Pepsi-Cola Co.	11.4	12.4	8.3	8.6	4.13
Gerber Products Co.	15.1	16.9	12.0	12.7	2.32
Green Giant Co.	8.6	10.2	7.1	7.7	3.61

Note: P_1 is aftertax income plus interest divided by book net worth plus long-term debt.

P_2 is aftertax income divided by book net worth.

$P_1{}^*$ is corrected net income plus interest divided by corrected net worth plus long-term debt.

$P_2{}^*$ is corrected net income divided by corrected net worth.

Source: Harry Bloch, "Advertising Profitability: A Reappraisal," *Journal of Political Economy,* vol. 82, no. 2 (March/April 1974), p. 285.

Table C-2
ESTIMATED ADVERTISING RETENTION RATE, ADVERTISING INTENSITY, ACCOUNTING RATE OF RETURN, AND CORRECTED RATE OF RETURN BY FIRM, 1968

Firm	Advertising Retention Rates (estimated)	Advertising-to-Sales Ratio	Accounting Rates of Return	Corrected Rates of Return
Alberto-Culver	.872	26.53	23.93	9.57
Borden	.632	2.36	7.61	7.35
Bristol-Myers	.913	16.59	19.40	12.88
Campbell Soup	.632	5.77	12.32	10.64
Carnation	.632	3.96	13.88	13.45
Carter-Wallace	.872	27.83	11.16	8.75
Chesebrough-Ponds	.872	11.97	20.28	9.99
Chrysler	.949	1.34	14.07	10.29
CPC International	.632	6.23	12.52	11.03
Firestone	.853	2.25	12.57	11.44
Ford	.949	1.46	12.67	9.60
General Electric	.876	1.17	14.32	10.93
General Foods	.632	10.16	14.20	11.88
General Mills	.632	6.89	12.58	11.29
General Motors	.949	1.23	17.75	13.34
Gillette	.872	19.09	28.15	16.66
B. F. Goodrich	.853	2.24	7.61	7.36
Goodyear	.853	2.28	12.75	11.92
Heinz	.632	5.01	10.25	10.40
Johnson & Johnson	.913	5.05	14.41	11.02
Kellogg	.632	16.40	20.33	12.68
Kraftco	.632	2.64	11.24	9.87
Miles Labs.	.913	22.90	12.48	6.96
Nabisco	.632	7.16	15.24	12.21
Noxell	.872	38.58	17.22	12.05
Pfizer	.872	8.27	13.89	13.85
Pillsbury	.632	6.97	10.36	9.13
Plough	.913	24.65	21.79	17.69
Quaker Oats	.632	5.75	12.50	9.03
Ralston-Purina	.632	2.29	11.86	10.02
RCA	.876	2.75	16.45	14.77
Revlon	.872	10.03	16.54	9.61
Richardson-Merrell	.913	20.72	11.98	9.51
Smith, Kline & French	.913	10.02	23.69	19.23
Standard Brands	.632	7.70	12.95	11.40
Sterling Drug	.913	20.93	18.70	10.86
Uniroyal	.853	2.43	11.40	10.34
Warner-Lambert	.913	15.11	17.88	13.86
Westinghouse	.876	1.62	10.51	8.67

Source: Robert Ayanian, "Advertising and Rate of Return," *Journal of Law and Economics,* vol. 18, no. 2 (October 1975), p. 499.

Table C-3
ACCOUNTING AND ESTIMATED CORRECTED RATES
OF RETURN FOR SIX DRUG FIRMS, 1973
(in percentages)

Firm	Accounting Rate of Return	Corrected Rate of Return	
		When ARD[a] depreciation rate is 13 percent	When ARD[a] depreciation rate is 9 percent
Abbott Laboratories	14.12	11.47	11.20
Eli Lilly and Company	21.30	16.45	16.00
Pfizer	15.90	13.62	13.34
Richardson-Merrell	13.91	12.19	12.06
G. D. Searle and Company	21.94	17.72	17.23
Upjohn Company	19.03	12.89	12.32
Six-firm average	17.70	14.06	13.69

[a] Advertising, research, and development.
Source: Robert Ayanian, "The Profit Rates and Economic Performance of Drug Firms," in *Drug Development and Marketing*, ed. by R. Helms (Washington, D.C.: American Enterprise Institute for Public Policy Research, 1975), p. 89.

uses a single life cycle for advertising, research, and development outlays. This contrasts with the present study, which uses a three-year life cycle for advertising, a different life cycle for research, and another for development, with these also varying among industries. Table C-3 shows the accounting and estimated corrected rates of return for pharmaceutical firms for both 13 percent and 9 percent advertising and research and development depreciation.

There are other differences between this and the Ayanian study of the rate of return in pharmaceutical firms. For example, Ayanian compares the corrected rates of return to the uncorrected median rate of return in the *Fortune* 500 sample. The present study corrects other industry rates of return before making comparisons with the pharmaceutical industry rate of return. The present study also avoids the possibility that disequilibrium or cyclical forces may distort relative returns by averaging returns over a period longer than the typical business cycle. This procedure eliminates some of the cyclical factors and permits some (although not a complete) averaging of temporary disequilibrium forces. It does not, however, eliminate the biases that might occur for industries which are on their way down toward a competitive equilibrium rate of return and those on their way up toward a competitive equilibrium rate of return. Relative to the unbiased rates of return, the former will show higher averages in the industry rates of return and the latter lower averages in the industry rate of return during the period investigated.

While each of these studies uses different methods for correcting rates of return and alternative data sources, the results they obtain are clear and strong—namely, that accounting rates of return in firms with intangible capital are biased upward.

Cover and book design: Pat Taylor